puff

50 flaky, crunchy, delicious appetizers, entrées, and desserts made with PUFF PASTRY

by Martha Holmberg

photographs by Ngoc Minh Ngo

CHRONICLE BOOKS

SAN FRANCISCO

To **Charlotte Umanoff** and **Craig Umanoff**, my daughter and my husband. Thank you, darlings, you are the best tasters, thinkers, listeners, and supporters ever.

Library of Congress Cataloging-in-Publication Data:
Holmberg, Martha.
  Puff : 50 flaky, crunchy, delicious appetizers, entrées, and desserts made with puff pastry / by Martha Holmberg ; photographs by Ngoc Minh Ngo.
    p. cm.
  ISBN: 978-0-8118-5952-3
  1. Pastry. I. Title.
  TX773.H625 2008
  641.8'65—dc22

                            2008008968

Manufactured in China.

Designed by **Alice Chau**.

Prop stylist: **Ngoc Minh Ngo**
Food stylist: **Poukè**
Food stylist assistant: **Anne Christina Milne**

Photographer's acknowledgments:
I'd like to thank Martha for her wonderful puff-pastry-making demonstrations and inspiring recipes.

10 9 8 7 6 5 4 3 2 1

Chronicle Books LLC
680 Second Street
San Francisco, California 94107

www.chroniclebooks.com

table of contents

why i love puff pastry

When I started this cookbook, I was quite fond of puff pastry and used it regularly, though not frequently, in my home cooking. I had enjoyed making it back in my days as a cooking school student and then a private chef in Paris, but nonetheless, I expected to end up hating the stuff after developing and testing so many recipes for this book. To my surprise, I am now an even more passionate fan of puff pastry. It has so much going for it: it's fun to make and easy to use, it works in a million different dishes, and it makes everyone who eats it very happy.

Once you have your pastry dough in hand—whether you make it from scratch (which is time-consuming but a blast in a pastry-geek kind of way) or use store-bought—puff pastry is a cinch to work with. It's surprisingly not that delicate, it isn't sticky, and you can refreeze the scraps. Plus, it's so darn versatile, even more now that I've discovered that in addition to baking it, you can fry it, with mind-blowingly delicious results.

Unlike flaky pie dough, which is mostly homey, or *pâte sucrée*, which is mostly prissy and precise, puff pastry can be as fancy as **Wild Salmon in Pastry with Savory Mushroom Stuffing and Lemon-Caper Beurre Blanc** (page 86) or as rustic as **Provençal Pizza** (page 69). And it adapts marvelously to dishes that traditionally use other types of pastry, such as Greek phyllo or Moroccan *briq*.

YOUR CHOICE:
store-bought, classic, or something in between

Frozen puff pastry is the ultimate convenience food—a package in the freezer means chic hors d'oeuvres or a homey galette can be under way in less than an hour. Most readers will find that store-bought pastry is a great place to start honing your skills. If you're a fanatic, however, making your own puff pastry from scratch is both a challenge and a thrill, and once you've made a batch, you can roll it, freeze it, and enjoy the instant gratification of frozen pastry later. For the hurried cook who still likes to get her hands in the dough, **Rough Puff Pastry** (page 30) is a brilliant middle ground. This dough takes just minutes to mix (and a bit more resting/chilling time), and while it doesn't deliver the sky-high results of true puff pastry, it offers all the same buttery, flaky charm.

To understand the anatomy of puff pastry and what makes it so darn flaky, see the discussion on page 22.

For speed and convenience, nothing beats commercial frozen puff pastry. The brand that you'll find just about everywhere is Pepperidge Farm (*www.puffpastry.com*). It's in the freezer section, of course, usually near the frozen pies and cakes. Each box contains two folded sheets of pastry, weighing just under 9 ounces each. The

downside of Pepperidge Farm is that it's made with vegetable shortening instead of butter, meaning that the flavor is relatively bland and I don't think it keeps as well as butter pastry once cooked. A minor upside is that it's vegan, so some of the recipes in the book will work for vegans, too.

I've developed all the recipes in this book using Pepperidge Farm puff pastry, simply because it is so available and affordable, and it's extremely easy to handle. However, you can use other commercial brands or homemade rough or classic puff pastry for any of the recipes; an explanation of how to substitute follows.

A fine brand of frozen all-butter puff pastry that's available in many parts of the country is from Dufour Pastry Kitchens (*www.dufourpastry kitchens.com*). A 1-pound sheet of pastry comes in an aluminum container with a cardboard cover (like a frozen lasagna). You can substitute a half-sheet of Dufour for one sheet of Pepperidge Farm. The Dufour will be a tiny bit thinner when you roll it to the specified dimensions, but that shouldn't be a problem.

Trader Joe's has its own brand of frozen all-butter puff pastry, which is quite tasty (Trader Joe's is a quirky specialty food chain that's in about half the country). And I've also found frozen puff pastry at my local international foods store (both all-butter and shortening versions) in 5-inch squares, which are great for making the **Parmesan-Paprika Twists** (page 34), **Martini Straws** (page 43), and other recipes in this book that use small sections of pastry. Your local markets may carry other brands, and you may even have a bakery that will sell you its own puff pastry dough to use at home, so be on the lookout for products that suit your needs.

The key is to know the weight of the dough and to cut it to the approximate weight called for in my recipe. That way, when you roll to the specific dimensions of the recipe, the thickness should be correct.

The same principle applies to puff pastry from scratch. The **Classic Puff Pastry** (page 26) and **Rough Puff Pastry** (page 30) recipes in this book each make just over 1 pound of dough, so you can make the full recipe and have the equivalent of two sheets of Pepperidge Farm, whether you cut it in half or leave it whole. If whatever dough you use is a little bit different in quantity than what I've called for in the recipe, the only thing you really need to watch is the cooking time. If your dough is a tad thinner, it will cook more quickly; thicker, it will need more time and, perhaps, a slightly lower oven temperature.

YOU NEED TO KNOW THIS! techniques
for getting the most from your dough

While baked puff pastry is ethereal, the unbaked dough is easygoing and a breeze to work with. It'll be even breezier if you mind these tips:

THAWING FROZEN DOUGH PROPERLY IS SO IMPORTANT

When thawing from-scratch dough to be rolled and shaped, allow an overnight thaw in the fridge for best results; this will permit the dough to be the same temperature and firmness all the way through the block. If the dough is too hard, you'll find yourself wrangling it a bit too vigorously in order to roll it out, and all you'll do is crush the layers or make it elastic and hard to shape.

When thawing commercial frozen pastry that's already in sheets (such as Pepperidge Farm), an overnight thaw is also a great idea, but 45 minutes to an hour on the counter, still wrapped, works fine too. The most important thing is DO NOT TRY TO UNFOLD THE SHEET IF THE PASTRY IS TOO COLD, or you'll crack it along the folds **A**. My testers had this problem over and over until they got the message: don't rush it.

If cracks do occur, however, don't worry; they can be fixed. Simply let the dough fully soften, then push the dough together with your fingertips along the seam and then pat to smooth the surface **B**. If the cracking seems severe, flip the sheet of dough and repeat with the seam on that side, too.

If you let the dough get too warm, the folded layers can fuse together and unfolding becomes a

Unfolding frozen pastry before it's fully thawed will cause the sheet to split—something you definitely don't want.

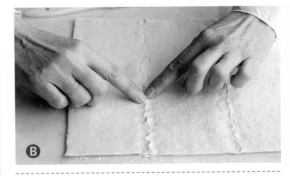

If cracks do happen, you can fix them. First let the pastry thaw completely, then push the dough together along the seams with your fingertips.

problem. But be patient and try to coax the layers apart; once the edge separates, the rest of the sheet unfolds easily.

If any beads of moisture have condensed on the pastry during thawing, gently blot them with a paper towel before rolling.

ROLLING THE DOUGH EVENLY NEEDS YOUR ATTENTION

Puff pastry is generally quite easy to roll out, as long as your kitchen's not too hot and you use enough flour on your work surface. Lightly flour the counter before you lay out your dough. Start to roll, and if the dough feels sticky, lightly flour the upper side and your pin also. After every few strokes of the rolling pin, lift up the edges of the dough and slide the whole sheet around a bit to be sure it's not adhering to the counter. If you sense it sticking, flop it over and dust the counter again with flour. I like to flip my sheet of dough a few times during rolling to keep the pressure even.

I think you get the best results when you roll along the vertical axis only, meaning straight up and down in front of you, and not side to side; so if you're trying to roll a square or circle, turn the pastry, not your rolling pin. Do not roll over the ends of the dough, because that will taper them and make your sheet of dough thinner at the edge than in the middle; you want one even sheet from end to end.

If your dough starts getting wonky as you roll, use your hands or a bench knife to pat it back into an even shape. You can roll it from side to side or stretch it gently in a few spots if necessary, but beware: dough that's stretched too much will rebel by shrinking back in the oven, so it's not the best method for shaping.

After you've rolled your desired shape, be sure to sweep off all excess flour with a clean, dry pastry brush.

Here's a great tip: I have noticed that sometimes, especially when the dough was warmish, my beautiful rectangle of dough would begin to resemble an hourglass, with the middle narrow and both ends flaring. You can avoid this with a simple trick: As you roll the dough lengthwise, only roll the top and bottom thirds of the dough, leaving the center alone, and therefore thicker. Then, turn the dough 90 degrees and roll normally; the excess will now fill out the narrow center.

CUTTING CLEAN, UNIFORM SHAPES IS A MATTER OF TECHNIQUE

You need to cut puff pastry very precisely in order to have neat shapes and evenly rising edges, so use either a long, sharp chef's knife with a single, smooth downward stroke, like an old-fashioned paper cutter, or a pizza wheel and a straightedge. To cut circles, use pastry cutters for small shapes and something like a pie pan or pot lid as a template, and cut around it with the tip of a sharp paring knife held upright.

Real pastry chefs like to flip the pastry over when they put it on the baking sheet, so the side that was on the bottom when they cut it is now on the top. The theory is that the layers that are on the bottom during cutting get slightly crushed and fused together, and by flipping them to the top, the whole piece will rise more evenly. Feel free to use this practice, but I haven't noticed much difference so I don't usually bother. Sometimes, though, it's fun to act like a French pastry chef and do it anyway.

MOVING THE DOUGH FROM WORK SURFACE TO BAKING SHEET IS SIMPLE WHEN YOU UNROLL

Pick up rolled-out dough with your hands and you risk stretching and deforming it, so once your dough is shaped, try not to touch it much. To move small shapes, I'll slide my bench knife or a wide spatula underneath and transfer them to the baking sheet. For larger rectangles or circles, I'll place the rolling pin at one edge, curl the pastry over the pin, and loosely roll it up **C**; then, I use the pin to transfer it to the baking sheet and gently unfurl it into position **D**. This neat trick works for any kind of pastry.

To move large pieces of dough, let the pin do the work. Loosely roll the dough around the rolling pin . . .

. . . then position the pin over your baking sheet and unroll the dough. This method avoids stretching and tearing.

PREPPING THE BAKING SHEET— DON'T BOTHER, REALLY

For most recipes, you need do nothing to the baking sheet but make sure it's clean and smooth. If you want to use nonstick, you can, but it's not necessary because puff pastry just isn't very sticky. It does shrink during baking, however, especially when it's been rolled very thin (because the gluten in the flour develops and becomes elastic). When you want your rolled-out dough to keep a perfect shape, moisten the baking sheet with a spritz of water, which "grabs" the pastry and helps prevent movement.

JOINING PIECES OF PASTRY IS BEST WITH WATER

I've seen so many recipes that call for using beaten egg as the "glue" for joining pieces of puff pastry, such as when you're stacking pieces to create a higher border or pinching together the edges of a triangular turnover. But in my experience, egg just makes things slippery. Plain water works better and is less of a hassle, too. I fill a small bowl with lukewarm water, dip my finger in it, and run my finger along the edge of the pastry. Light pressure is enough when you're

stacking layers, but I press the edges of turnovers together like I really mean it, because they tend to puff open no matter what.

GLAZING, ONLY WHEN YOU FEEL FRANÇAISE

To be really French, we should probably be brushing all our puff pastries with an egg wash, but that's a step I happily skip in most cases. You'll see a few recipes in this book in which I brush the pastry with some kind of glaze—egg, melted butter, or perhaps cream—but I do that mostly as a way of getting other ingredients to stick to it, such as the coarse sugar on the **Gingery Peach Berry Galette** (page 106). In a couple of cases, I've called for an egg glaze to "dress up" the finished pastry, but even that is optional.

CONTROLLING THE PUFF DEPENDS ON YOUR ULTIMATE GOAL

The best way to get an even rise from puff pastry is to make the dough correctly, roll it out gently without forcing, cut it cleanly, and bake it in an oven that's hot enough. But while we go to great lengths to create a pastry that will climb like a skyscraper on the Singapore skyline, in some recipes you need to control or even restrict the height. Two techniques can help you get the degree of loft you want: if you're using puff pastry as a base for a tart or galette, a very puffy center means there's no room for the filling, so the recipe will instruct you to prick the pastry all over with a fork. This is called "docking" the pastry. (You can buy a roller docker—like a wicked-looking paint roller—if you want to get hardcore about it 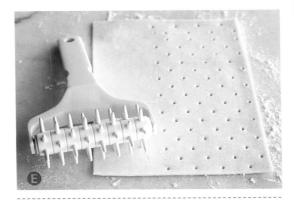.) For the **Quick Chocolate-Raspberry Napoleons** (page 124) and **S'Mores** (page 121), you want the pastry as flat and waferlike as you can get, while still being flaky and crisp, so you'll roll the pastry very thin, and then weight it down with another baking sheet or an inverted

cooling rack. This allows the dough to cook thoroughly but prevents puffing.

There's a third technique that's worth knowing, if only because the name is so cool and fun to say—*chiqueter* (pronounced SHE cuh tay). This subtle edge crimping can help knit two layers of dough together and also—in theory anyway—guide the pastry to a more even vertical rise. To chiqueter the pastry, you hold a table or paring knife upright and, with the blunt back edge, make indentations along the pastry edge about a quarter to a half inch apart . This also gives the pastry a nice finished look. I only call for this in a couple of recipes, but you could do it on any pastry that wants a tailored look.

Sometimes you don't want your pastry to puff too much. Pricking the surface will give you a controlled, even rise. You can use a fork or a special roller-docker to get the job done quickly.

A special crimping method, called *chiquetere*, creates neat borders that rise evenly. With the back edge of a knife, make evenly spaced indentations; this stitches the pastry together.

GETTING THE OVEN TEMPERATURE RIGHT MEANS STARTING EARLY

My standard oven temperature for puff pastry is 400°F. But setting your oven to that number is meaningless unless you know your oven is true. If you don't already have one, get yourself an oven thermometer to be sure you're on track. If not, most ovens can be easily calibrated following the instructions in the user's manual. Personally, I'm incapable of reading an owner's manual, so I'd just adjust the dial up or down a bit to compensate! It is absolutely imperative that your oven is hot enough when you start baking the pastry. Puff pastry needs an immediate hit of high heat to create the burst of steam that separates and puffs the layers, and if that doesn't happen, the fat will melt and seep out of the layers, leaving you with a denser result. So please allow plenty of time for heating up, which is generally more time than your oven display panel tells you. I give mine at least 20 minutes and up to 30 minutes to be sure it's evenly hot.

In some recipes in this book, I call for a lower temperature, generally when the pastry is rolled fairly thick and needs time for the heat to penetrate. If the temperature is too high, the outside gets browned before the interior is cooked through. In other cases, it's because the pastry has a wet filling that needs thorough cooking, such as the frangipane in the **Oregon Berry Tartlets** (page 108). A few recipes get baked at 425°F when I want the filling to simply warm up while the pastry browns.

And here's where I ask each cook to use personal judgment. Trust your eyes, nose, and palate more than the clock. No matter how scrupulous you are about following a recipe, there are always variables that will affect cooking time, such as ambient temperature, type of baking sheet, oven performance, phase of the moon, whatever. So, the times in the recipes are simply guidelines; far more important are the doneness descriptions. Don't worry if your dish needs more or less time to get to the desired state; what really matters is the final result, not how many minutes you baked it.

BLIND BAKING FOR A CRISP BOTTOM MAKES TARTS TASTIER

Getting dough evenly crisp and brown is a challenge for any type of pastry, and puff pastry can be even trickier because it has a fairly high moisture content. For deep-dish tarts and quiches,

I suggest blind baking first, to give the bottom crust a chance at drying out and browning before the wet filling takes over. You'll never achieve a perfectly crisp bottom, but at least it won't be soggy. Instructions for blind baking are included in the relevant recipes.

GETTING AHEAD—YOU'VE GOT OPTIONS

The best way to get ahead with puff pastry is to roll and shape your pastries, and then freeze them raw. They can go directly from freezer to oven; just add a few more minutes of cooking time. For shapes to be deep-fried, such as the **Profiteroles with Coffee Cream, Rich Chocolate-Espresso Sauce, and Toasted Almonds** (page 131), let the pastry shapes thaw a few minutes, otherwise they may burn on the outside before they're totally cooked inside. Some of the dishes here reheat quite well, such as the **Ham, Gruyère, and Dijon Palmiers** (page 35) and the **Brown Sugar and Brandy Pear Turnovers** (page 109), but the ideal for any puff pastry dish is to be eaten shortly after cooking.

a quick conversation about ingredients

As any good cook knows, a recipe is only as good as the ingredients you use, so the cooking process really starts in the grocery store or farmers' market. Most of the recipes in this book call for ingredients that you can get at any reasonable grocery store, but I have snuck in a couple (such as smoked paprika and Spanish chorizo) that you may need to get from a specialty store or online source. To make sure you'll have what you need, read your recipe thoroughly before you embark on it.

In general, I'm all for improvisation and substitution—just because a recipe tells you to use one thing, doesn't mean you can't try it with something you like better or have on hand—but there are certain fundamental ingredients about which I have strong feelings. Please read the following advice about a few frequently used components of the recipes in this book.

BUTTER

For the right butter to use to make the puff pastry from scratch, see my discussion on page 20. When the butter is for anything else, use whatever you've got on hand. I've developed the recipes with unsalted butter just for consistency's sake,

but to be honest, I prefer salted butter because I'm kind of a salt freak, and that's usually what I have on hand in the fridge. In most recipes in this book, the difference in final flavor is negligible, and you'll be salting to taste anyway.

FRESH HERBS

I use fresh herbs in practically everything I cook; it's second nature to me, so I'm always surprised when I talk to cooks who don't. It's true that when you buy herbs in the store (as opposed to having your own herb garden), it can get expensive, but if you store herbs correctly, they'll last a week or more, and surely you can find a good use for a sprig of thyme or a handful of cilantro, no? I like to wrap my leafy herbs—such as parsley, cilantro, and mint—in a barely damp paper towel and then put them in a plastic storage box in the fridge. For the heartier herbs—thyme and rosemary— I stand them up in a small, empty vase on my counter and let them dry gently. Basil is tricky, because it doesn't like the low temperature of the fridge and will turn black easily. The best solution is to fill a glass with cold water, put the bunch of basil in it like a bouquet of flowers, cover loosely with a plastic bag, and keep it on the counter, using it up as quickly as you can.

LEMON ZEST

A hint of freshly grated lemon zest is often what's needed to lift the flavors in a dish. I frequently add it just to create balance rather than to make something taste lemony. And the only way to grate zest well is with a rasp-style grater (see page 17). When grated this way, you'll get about 2 teaspoons lightly packed zest from a 4-ounce lemon.

OLIVE OIL

I love olive oil, I live on olive oil, it's the only oil I keep on hand, and I use it for everything, including frying my daughter's French toast in the morning. I like to have two kinds to choose from: a relatively cheap extra-virgin for cooking (I often use Colavita, which I think has a mild, lightly fruity flavor) and a more expensive oil for "finishing," that is, drizzling on bean soups, salads, and pastas. A good bet that doesn't blow the bank is Unio from Spain, which is assertive but not super peppery. The most important thing for any oil, including neutral varieties such as canola and safflower (which you'll need for the fried pastry recipes in this book), is freshness. All oils get rancid when exposed to heat, light, and oxygen, so keep them tightly capped and in a cupboard, and only buy what you can consume in a month or two. And always taste your oil when you first break the seal, as a point of reference, and then taste again every time you use it. When it starts to taste funny, ditch it and get a fresh bottle.

PARMESAN CHEESE

You'll notice Parmesan cheese in a lot of my recipes. I must go through a pound a week at home, and it's definitely the food I'd want on a desert island (well, it might come in second, after a slice of buttered toast made from a loaf of *filoni* from Sullivan Street Bakery in New York). By "Parmesan," however, I mean true imported Parmigiano-Reggiano from Italy that you grate as you need it. None of the waxy grocery store stuff, please, and definitely nothing pre-grated. Imported Parmesan is not cheap, but it's definitely a good investment. You can get the real thing in most groceries now, and because it stores well, you can order it with confidence from an online source such as *www.igourmet.com* or *www.zingermans.com*.

Grana Padano is an OK second choice. Two ounces of Parmesan grated on a fine rasp-style grater (see page 17) will yield one cup, lightly packed.

SALT AND PEPPER

What could be more basic than this seasoning duo, but nowadays the cook has choices. I use kosher salt exclusively in cooking, mostly because I think it's a lot easier to control than a finer salt. My preferred brand is Diamond Crystal (in the red box), because it's pure salt (no anti-caking agents) and because the grains are coarse enough that they're easy to handle, yet they crush to a powder between your fingers, which I do when blending the salt into dry ingredients.

All my recipes here are developed with kosher salt, so if you use a finer salt, such as a fine sea salt or a table salt like Morton's, you'll need to add less salt. One tablespoon of Morton table salt is the same weight, and therefore the same amount of salt, as 2 tablespoons of Diamond Crystal kosher. In most recipes, you'll be able to taste and adjust. As for pepper, I have a pepper mill filled with Tellicherry peppercorns that I grind to order. Unlike salt, which is essentially inert and doesn't lose flavor, pepper needs to be ground fresh to capture its complex and wonderful flavor. If you're still using preground pepper, now's the time to start grinding your own.

tools that make life easier

It's a poor craftsman who blames his tools, but a very clever one who selects cool tools that make the job much easier. It goes without saying that a good cook needs good pots and pans, sharp knives, and proper measuring tools, but there are a few specific items that make puff-pastry baking easier. Here are the utensils I think you need for success with my recipes.

BAKING SHEETS

I use simple aluminum 13-by-18-inch baking sheets with a rim, also called half-sheet pans, for just about all my baking. They're sturdy, inexpensive, and good heat conductors. The rim is low enough to allow good browning, yet it will contain any drips from fillings. Most other types of baking sheets are fine, too, as long as they're thick enough not to warp in the heat of the oven. I do not, however, recommend an insulated sheet pan (such as Cushion Air brand) for anything larger than small pastry shells, because I think it prevents pastry from browning properly. Know, also, that a dark pan will brown pastry faster than a light-colored one.

BENCH KNIFE

This is a handy tool for cutting butter, cutting dough, and scraping dough from your work surface. A bench knife is a flat metal rectangle topped with a wooden or plastic handle. Mine has inches marked on the edge so it serves as a ruler, too. A variant is a pastry scraper, which is usually a stiff plastic card that cuts and scrapes, though not with the authority of a bench knife.

GRATER

If you do only one thing that I suggest in this section, this is what it should be: Buy a rasp-style grater! It will truly change your life (the brand you'll most often find is Microplane). Those of you who already have one know exactly what I'm talking about. The super-sharp, fine teeth make zesting citrus—which in the past was literally a pain, between scraped knuckles and digging the bits of zest from the teeth of a box grater—a delight. Once you start "rasping," you'll want to add lemon zest to everything, which is a good thing because I use a lot in this book—it's such a flavor-lifter. And grating Parmesan is a dream; you'll create mounds of fluffy cheese in seconds. All my measurements for these two ingredients are based on using a rasp-style grater, so that's another good reason to get one.

PARCHMENT PAPER

Unlike many pastries, puff pastry obligingly does not stick (provided your baking sheet is clean and smooth), so you don't need parchment paper or a baking mat. In some recipes with a sticky or juicy filling, however, I instruct you to use a liner for easy cleanup.

PASTRY BRUSHES

It's important, while rolling out your dough, to use enough flour to prevent sticking. However, you don't want that flour to actually be incorporated into the dough, so a decisive sweep each time you roll will brush away the excess. Have at least two or three brushes: Reserve one just for pastry-making and have another one or two for brushing with butter or egg wash. I tend to buy cheap brushes so that I can throw them away when they start to get gunky.

ROLLING PINS

To me, the most important feature of a rolling pin is how it feels in your hands. I get more control from my straight, French-style pin (with no handles), but that's probably just because I've used it for so long. I bought mine at the Parisian cookware shop Dehillerin when I was a cooking student in the late 1980s and have toted it throughout my many moves. Puff pastry isn't fragile, as a rich *pâte sucrée* might be, so there's no need for fancy silicone or chillable rolling pins.

STRAIGHTEDGE

Just about every recipe in this book lists a specific measurement to which you roll the pastry, so having a designated kitchen ruler that's at least 18 inches long is a good idea. You can use it to guide your knife or pizza cutter in order to make a straight cut, too. Other tools are handy for cutting even pieces of pastry; I've seen a pastry chef use a drywall float as a straightedge, which is brilliant because the handle allows you to position it steadily on the pastry as you cut. But, please, buy one just for pastry work, don't go rummaging through the garage.

MAKING puff pastry FROM scratch

While *pâte feuilletée* may be at the top of the fancy heap of French pastries, this classic puff pastry really is achievable for a home cook. The only special skill you need is a talent for waiting—puff pastry demands lots of intervals for resting and chilling, and if you try to skip or rush them, especially when you're first learning, you'll get into trouble.

But before you break out the butter, let's take a minute to study the basics, because once you understand the theory, the practice will be a lot easier.

CHOOSING the right ingredients

AIM FOR LOWER PROTEIN IN YOUR FLOUR

I use a mix of all-purpose flour and cake flour. I've developed these recipes using Gold Medal unbleached all-purpose flour, which has a medium amount of protein. I reduce that even more by blending in the cake flour, which is really low in protein, giving me a flour that won't be too high in gluten (read on to learn why that's important). If you use a brand such as King Arthur, with a high protein content, you might substitute a tablespoon or two with more cake flour.

USE FRESH BUTTER WITH LOW WATER CONTENT

Puff pastry is really all about the butter, so the better the butter, the better the pastry. Good butter means fresh butter, so nothing that's lingered long enough in the fridge to pick up odors or to oxidize a bit (which causes a darkening of the outer layer). Ideally, choose a butter with a high fat content. Surprisingly, butter isn't all butterfat; many brands contain up to 18 percent water. European-style butters, such as Plugra, have low water content and are easier to use because they're very "plastic" and will spread nicely under the force of the rolling pin without breaking. Land O'Lakes is a good mass-market option. Unsalted is best, because that's what these recipes were developed with, but truth be told, I use salted butter in my baking frequently because I love highly salted food.

handling your ingredients FOR SUCCESS

MEASURING FLOUR FOR CONSISTENCY

The next few sentences contain possibly the most important information in this book. Please read! It's critical that you measure your flour accurately. Depending on the condition of your flour in the bag and the way you get the flour into your measuring cup, you could have anywhere between less than 4 or more than 5 ounces, and that discrepancy is the difference between perfect pastry and a sheet of cardboard.

The most reliable way to measure flour is by weighing it on a scale. I have included weights in parentheses in these from-scratch recipes. But not many American cooks use scales (pity, it makes life so easy), so here's how you need to measure your flour for these recipes. Use true dry measuring cups (not a measuring cup with a pour spout designed for liquids) and use the proper size so that you can fill to the brim rather than guesstimate. If you want ½ cup of flour, use a ½-cup measure rather than using a 1-cup measure and saying, "That's about halfway full." As flour sits on the shelf, it compacts, so first stir the flour in your bag to loosen it up a bit. Spoon the flour from the bag into your dry measuring cup,

then with the back of a knife, sweep off the excess so the flour is exactly level with the rim of the cup. When I do this with Gold Medal flour, I get a 4½-ounce cup. Cake flour is a tad lighter.

ADDING WATER BY FEEL, NOT BY THE NUMBERS

The ability of flour to absorb water varies depending on how humid the flour itself is, which is a function of storage and ambient humidity. This means you should always be a little wary of water amounts when making any kind of pastry. A good practice is to add about three-quarters of the specified amount first, then add more a few drops at a time until you get the right consistency. In some cases, you may need to add even more than the recipe calls for.

Doughs often seem a little dry at first, but as the flour absorbs and swells, the moisture evens out. I think it's better to start dry, and add a few drops of water as you start rolling the dough, rather than having a wet and sticky dough. If you do find yourself with a wet dough, just use a lot of flour on your work surface and rolling pin as you start to roll.

ANATOMY OF PUFF PASTRY

Puff pastry is a "laminated" dough, and indeed, the final dough is made of many fine layers sandwiched together. The layers alternate between pure butter and a layer made from a flour-and-water paste called a *détrempe* (day TROHMP).

But before we see how the lamination happens, we need a mini science lesson on gluten. Wheat flour contains proteins that, when moistened and/or kneaded, will develop into a substance called gluten. Gluten is both the friend and the enemy of puff pastry. Too little gluten and you won't get the fine flaky sheets characteristic of puff pastry, you'll just get crumbles (which is why we're not using all cake or pastry flour). But too much gluten makes the détrempe very elastic, which means it will shrink back annoyingly as you try to roll out the pastry and it messes up the butter distribution. Plus, an elastic dough is hard to shape and will be tough, not delicate, when baked.

You can inhibit excess gluten formation by adding an acid to your détrempe, such as lemon juice or a little white vinegar, and you can "shorten" the gluten, too, meaning to prevent it from forming long stretchy strands by mixing in fat (hence the terms "short crust," "shortbread," and vegetable "shortening"). To shorten the gluten when making puff pastry, I use a little melted butter in my détrempe.

walking through the method

YOUR FIRST STEP IS TO MAKE THE DÉTREMPE

The traditional ingredients are just flour, salt, and water, but for reasons I've just explained, I like to add lemon juice and a touch of melted butter, too. I handle the détrempe as little as possible in order to further limit gluten formation, so at first the ball of dough may appear bumpier and shaggier than you'd think is correct for puff pastry. But as you begin the rolling stages, everything smoothes out.

THE SECOND STEP IS TO GET THE BUTTER MALLEABLE

You want it soft enough so that it spreads out evenly as you roll it; if it's too hard, it will resist rolling and just stay in a lump, or it will fracture and you'll have gaps in the pastry with no butter. If it gets too soft, however, it will melt into the détrempe layer or squish out the ends of the pastry. I generally let my butter get fairly soft at room temperature, then I chill again until it's just firm enough for me to bend slightly without breaking. You should be able to make a depression when pressing hard with your finger, but only a shallow one.

Sometimes I'll work the butter by banging on it with my rolling pin and folding it on itself, like you would with modeling clay. You'll probably need to do this if you use sticks of butter, rather than a solid block (Plugra comes in a half-pound or 1-pound block).

THE THIRD STEP IS WRAPPING THE TWO TOGETHER

To start the layer formation, you wrap the butter in the détrempe so you now have three layers—dough/butter/dough. This is called the *paton*.

Now it's time for fun with math; this is how your lumpy little package of dough becomes tissue-thin layers of elegantly crisp pastry. You roll the paton to a long rectangle, and then fold it into thirds. So now your three layers become three layers of three, hence nine layers. You roll and fold again, giving you three layers of nine now. And so on, until you have 2,187 (if I've done the math right), which is kind of unbelievable. In actuality, you can't count that many layers once the pastry's baked because many have fused with each other during rolling and cooking, but a well-made puff pastry will have as many layers as anyone could possibly want.

TIPS ON ROLLING

When you roll out your puff pastry dough, keep in mind that you're rolling out layers of flour-and-water détrempe and layers of butter at the same time. You need to manipulate the dough so that both types of layers move at the same rate, otherwise your layer structure will suffer. When you begin to roll the block of dough, give it a head start by pressing down firmly and evenly with your rolling pin several times across the surface of the dough to flatten it slightly. This also softens up the butter a touch so that it's more responsive to the actual rolling.

When you roll, start from the middle and roll to one end, then place your pin back in the middle and roll to the other end. Only roll along one axis, from top to bottom, never from side to side unless you're making a small correction (more on that to follow). After every few strokes, I like to stop, loosen the dough from the counter, and then roll again. After every few sets, I'll flip the dough and roll on the other side.

Probably the most important aspect of rolling is to never let the dough get stuck to the counter. If it does, it won't be able to extend out under the pressure of the rolling pin—you'll be crushing the dough rather than stretching it out. You also risk ripping it and allowing the butter to leak out. So

the constant movement I just described is critical; my pastry chef at La Varenne cooking school used to encourage us to "dance with the dough," because the lifting and sliding motion looked sort of like we were jitterbugging with our pastry.

Don't be afraid of generously flouring your counter to prevent sticking also. It's better to work in a bit more flour than to struggle with a sticky dough and risk overworking it. Overworking the dough develops gluten and elasticity and will drive you right up the wall with frustration. So use plenty of flour, then brush off all the excess with a clean, dry pastry brush before you actually fold your length of dough.

Never roll over the ends of the dough because that would cause them to taper off and be thinner than the middle of the dough. You want one even sheet from end to end. As you roll, your sheet of dough may lose its geometric perfection, so use your hands or a bench knife to pat it back into an even rectangle. You can roll from side to side or stretch it gently in a few spots if necessary, but a dough that's stretched too much will rebel by shrinking back in the oven, so it's not the best method for shaping.

You'll be instructed at several points in the recipe to wrap and chill the pastry. This allows the gluten in the détrempe to relax and lets the butter firm up again. If at any time you feel the pastry is getting too soft—it becomes sticky or you see soft butter breaking through—or if you feel you're fighting elasticity, you should immediately slide it into the fridge again for 30 minutes or so. Low temperatures firm up the dough and relax the gluten, making the dough more supple and cooperative. And unless you're a true pro, don't even try making puff pastry on a hot, humid day unless your house is completely air-conditioned.

STORING THE PASTRY

Puff pastry stays happily in the fridge for a day or two, but beyond that, it tends to get gummy. But it loves the freezer, so if you want to make the dough ahead, just wrap it well in plastic and freeze, then thaw it in the fridge overnight.

YOUR CHOICE OF TWO STYLES

I'm including two from-scratch methods in this chapter: the classic, and a very quick version called rough puff pastry, or *demi-feuilletée* (half puff). Classic puff pastry is the premium version, giving an even, lofty rise and shatteringly crisp and delicate layers; mastering this pastry gives you a real sense of accomplishment. But as you can see from my lengthy discussion, it takes time and a certain amount of practice to

get truly perfect results. For many dishes—especially those where height is not the issue, such as quiches, galettes, turnovers, potpies—rough puff will be just as delicious and is much quicker to make.

Rough puff also uses the roll, fold, and turn technique, but instead of performing the operation on a dough that's made of three distinct layers, we do it with a shaggy jumble of butter and flour. What you end up with is not sheets of butter and dough but rather flat chips of butter scattered throughout a matrix of dough, like a terrazzo floor. Your layers may not be perfectly even and the rise won't be as high, but the pastry will still be endearingly flaky and buttery.

My advice is to start with the rough puff, which will give you practice with rolling and folding, then move up to classic. You'll soon learn which one you think is best for your style of cooking. The rough puff also freezes well. Both of these recipes can easily be doubled.

classic puff pastry *(pâte feuilletée)*

½ cup **ice water**

½ teaspoon **kosher salt**

½ teaspoon **fresh lemon juice**

2 tablespoons (1 ounce)
   unsalted butter, melted

½ cup (2 ounces) **cake flour**

1⅓ cups (6 ounces) **unbleached
   all-purpose flour**

14 tablespoons (7 ounces) cold
   unsalted butter

DO AHEAD

You can refrigerate the pastry dough for up
to one day or freeze it for up to two months.

Please note that for certain ingredients, I list measurements in two ways: first, by volume (cups, tablespoons); second, by weight. If you have a kitchen scale, you should weigh the flour; otherwise, measure the flour in a cup measure designed for dry ingredients (see **Measuring Flour for Consistency**, page 21).

MAKES ABOUT **1** POUND OF DOUGH

1 In a small bowl, stir the ice water, salt, lemon juice, and melted butter until the salt is dissolved. In another bowl, whisk together the cake and all-purpose flours, then dump them in a pile onto a counter, and with your hand, sweep away a large clearing in the center (called a "well"). Pour about three-quarters of the water mixture into the center of the well, and gradually mix in the flour by using your hand or a pastry scraper to scoot a few tablespoons at a time from the wall of the well into the center. With your fingers (use one hand only, or else things get too messy), mix the flour and liquid together to form a fairly

Start slowly and blend the water, salt, lemon juice, and melted butter with just enough flour to form a paste. As the paste gets smooth, flick in more flour and keep blending.

smooth paste **(A)**, then scoot in more flour, continuing until the dough starts to get thick and shaggy. At this point, use a bench knife or pastry scraper to lift, toss, and chop the dough into small bits so that the flour is evenly incorporated **(B)**. As the dough is coming together, add more of the water if it seems too dry. Add a few drops at a time, though you may not need to add all the water. Your goal is a dough that holds together without being too sticky and without visible spots of dry flour. This is called the détrempe.

2 Clean off your hands, then gently pat the dough into a rough ball. With your thumbs on top and other fingers underneath, turn the ball partly inside out, with the same gesture you'd use to break open a bread roll **(C)**; this brings the center of the dough, which is drier, closer to the surface. Gently pat the dough into a thick 5-inch round, and, using a sharp knife, score an X about ⅜ inch deep across the surface. Set the dough on a plate, cover with plastic, and refrigerate for 30 minutes.

CONTINUED >>

Use a pastry scraper or bench knife, tossing to get all the flour moistened, to form a shaggy dough without working the dough too much (which would develop gluten and make the dough too elastic).

Shape the dough into a rough ball, turn it partly inside out, which will flatten it a bit, then score the surface lightly to cut the gluten. Wrap it and let it rest so the flour fully hydrates and the dough relaxes.

Most American butter comes in sticks, so you'll need to pound it to fuse the sticks together to form a block.

3 If using a block of butter, pound it lightly with your rolling pin to get it malleable and shape it with your hands to form a square that's roughly 4 inches across. If using stick butter, pound the two sticks together to fuse them **D**, then shape into the 4-inch square **E**. Chill the butter for at least 30 minutes.

4 Take the détrempe and the butter from the refrigerator and gently poke them both with your finger to see whether they're of the same firmness. If the butter's too soft, chill again; if too firm, leave out for a few more minutes.

5 On a lightly floured counter, gently press and pat the détrempe to make a round that's about 10 inches across and is slightly thinner around the edges and mounded in the center. Put the butter block in the center and pull the edges up over the butter, pleating a bit as you go, to completely enclose the butter **F**. Press and pinch to make a neat and firmly sealed package, then flip the package over. By scootching

The trick is to keep the butter cool and unmelted, yet plastic and malleable. Pound it with a rolling pin, then shape it into a 4-inch square.

Wrap the dough around the butter, pleating and pressing to completely enclose it. This will be your first three layers—dough/butter/dough—so make the package neat.

your hands and pressing lightly with the rolling pin, shape the package so it's about 4 inches square. This is called the paton. If the paton feels sticky or soft, chill for 15 minutes before continuing.

6 With your rolling pin, gently but firmly press down on the paton with a few strokes across its surface to encourage it to expand, then roll the paton into about a 5-by-15-inch rectangle, lifting the dough after every few strokes to see if it's sticking. If it is, dust the surface lightly with more flour. After every few strokes, you should also loosen the dough from the counter so it can shrink back to its true size.

7 With a soft pastry brush, brush off any excess flour from the surface **G**, then fold the bottom third of the dough up and the top third down, like you're folding a letter. Make sure all the corners are square and all the edges of the dough line up neatly so the three layers are in perfect alignment. Turn the dough 90 degrees to the right, so that the long edge is on your left. This rolling, folding, and turning is called a "single turn" **H**.

8 Repeat the rolling and folding for one more single turn, neatening up the edges of the dough with your palms to keep them straight and snugging up the corners so they're square, as well as brushing off excess flour before you fold. Dust the block of pastry with more flour, wrap it in plastic, and chill for at least 30 minutes. Repeat for two more single turns; chill for another 30 minutes or more, and then finish with two more single turns. Chill for at least 30 minutes; the dough is now ready to roll out and shape.

Use enough flour so your dough doesn't stick to the counter as you roll. A quick cleanup with a dry pastry brush before each fold helps avoid working in too much flour.

Fold your dough neatly in thirds, to make a single turn. If you need to, gently tug the corners so that all three layers are evenly aligned.

rough puff pastry (*demi-feuilletée*)

1 cup (8 ounces) cold **unsalted butter**

1⅓ cups (6 ounces) **unbleached all-purpose flour**

½ cup **ice water**

½ teaspoon **fresh lemon juice**

½ teaspoon **kosher salt**

Please note that for certain ingredients, I list measurements in two ways: first, by volume (cups, tablespoons); second, by weight. If you have a kitchen scale, you should weigh the flour; otherwise, measure the flour in a cup measure designed for dry ingredients (see **Measuring Flour for Consistency**, page 21).

MAKES ABOUT **1** POUND OF DOUGH

1 Cut the butter into ½-inch cubes, spread out on a plate, and freeze for about 15 minutes.

2 MIXER METHOD: Combine the flour and the butter in a stand mixer fitted with the paddle attachment. Mix on low speed until the butter cubes are smashed up a bit and the chunks are about half their original size; don't worry if the chunks aren't uniform. Stir together the water, lemon juice, and salt until the salt is dissolved; then, with the mixer running, slowly pour the liquid mixture into the flour and butter and mix just until the dough barely holds together; it will look quite shaggy. Don't add all the liquid until you're sure you need it. The dough may seem a little dry at first, but it will come together as you start rolling.

2 HAND METHOD: Toss the flour and butter in a wide bowl and cut the butter into smaller pieces with a bench knife, pastry scraper, or table knife. Pinch and press the mixture with your fingers to encourage the butter to form flattened pieces. Stir together the water, lemon juice, and salt until the salt is dissolved, then gradually add the liquid mixture as you toss the flour mixture with a fork to evenly distribute the liquid. Your goal is a shaggy dough that just holds together.

DO AHEAD

You can refrigerate the dough for up to one day or freeze it for up to two months.

At first, rough puff dough seems impossible to roll because it's so crumbly, but don't give up.

3 Dump the dough onto a floured counter and pat it into a rough rectangle about 5 by 8 inches. Roll into a 5-by-15-inch rectangle **Ⓐ**, lifting the dough after every few rolls to be sure it's not sticking to the counter **Ⓑ** and dusting the counter with more flour if it is sticking.

4 With a soft pastry brush, brush off any excess flour from the surface, then fold the bottom third of the dough up and the top third down, like you're folding a letter **Ⓒ**. Make sure all the corners are square and all the edges of the dough line up neatly so the three layers are in perfect alignment. Turn the dough 90 degrees to the right, so that the open edge is on your left. This rolling, folding, and turning is called a "single turn."

5 Repeat the rolling and folding for three more single turns, each time neatening up the edges of the dough with your palms to keep them straight and snugging up the corners so they're square, as well as brushing off excess flour before you fold. Dust the block of pastry with more flour, wrap it in plastic, and chill for at least 30 minutes.

6 Repeat for two final single turns, then chill at least another 30 minutes before rolling and baking.

Use a bench knife to help keep the edges straight and to lift the dough off the counter when it's time to make a turn.

Gently fold the dough in thirds to form a single turn. After you've completed 2 or 3 turns, the dough gets much smoother and more workable.

LIGHT AND
CRUNCHY
appetizers
AND
snacks

parmesan-paprika twists

1 cup (about 2 ounces) freshly and finely grated **Parmesan cheese**

¼ teaspoon **smoked paprika**

¼ teaspoon **kosher salt**

⅛ teaspoon **cayenne pepper**

1 sheet (about 9 ounces) **frozen puff pastry**, thawed

1 **large egg**, beaten with a few drops of **water** and a pinch of **salt**

DO AHEAD

These are definitely best if freshly baked but can be stored in an airtight container for up to one day. Refresh in a 350°F oven for about 5 minutes.

These homemade cheese straws deliver a level of crunch that no snack from a box can match. Light and flaky, laced with salty cheese, and made intriguing with just a hint of heat, they're the perfect partner for an ice-cold martini or a glass of pinot noir. The twists look great on the table when you pile them into a tall tumbler.

MAKES **48** FIVE-INCH TWISTS

1 Heat the oven to 375°F. In a small bowl, toss the Parmesan, paprika, salt, and cayenne. On a lightly floured counter, roll the pastry sheet into a 10-by-12-inch rectangle. Cut it lengthwise to make two 5-by-12-inch strips. Brush the strips evenly with the beaten egg and spread the filling over both strips, making sure you come to the edges. Lightly press the filling so it sticks onto the pastry.

2 With a large chef's knife or a pizza cutter, cut each strip crosswise into twenty-four ½-inch strips. Pick up a strip, twist it two times, and lay it on a baking sheet, pressing the ends lightly into the sheet to keep it from untwisting. Continue with all the strips. If any cheese falls off, scoop it up and sprinkle over the twists.

3 Bake until the twists are puffed, light brown, and no longer doughy, about 15 minutes (taste one to make sure it's dry all the way through). Let cool on a rack and serve within an hour or two.

34

ham, gruyère, and dijon palmiers

These hors d'oeuvres are flaky, chewy, and impossibly good with a chilled glass of Riesling. The *palmier* (PAHL me yay) is a classic shape in French pastry that's easy to form and that shows off fillings beautifully. Here, I layer mustard, ham, and Gruyère cheese with the pastry, so the flavors are classic, too. Get the ham sliced very thinly at the deli counter. If the ham falls apart a bit, that's okay; you can piece it together as you assemble the palmiers.

------------------ MAKES **24** PALMIERS --------------------

1 sheet (about 9 ounces) **frozen puff pastry**, thawed

2 tablespoons **Dijon mustard**

About 1 cup (3 ounces) grated **aged Gruyère cheese**

¼ cup (½ ounce) freshly and finely grated **Parmesan cheese**

4 ounces very thinly sliced **good-quality baked ham**, such as Black Forest

1 Position the sheet of pastry on a lightly floured counter so that a short side is closest to you. Roll the pastry into a 10-by-14-inch rectangle. Trim the edges, if necessary, to make the rectangle neat.

2 Using the back of a spoon or an offset spatula, spread the mustard over the pastry. Distribute the Gruyère and Parmesan evenly over the surface. Arrange the ham in a single even layer, tearing or cutting pieces to fit. Lay a piece of parchment paper or waxed paper on top and gently compress the layers with the rolling pin. Peel off the paper without disturbing the ham.

3 Cut the rectangle in half widthwise to make two 10-by-7-inch bands. With your fingers, gently roll one short edge of one of the bands into the center and then roll the opposite edge in so the two rolls meet in the middle and resemble a double scroll. Press lightly so the rolls stick together (spread a few drops of water where the two rolls meet to help

CONTINUED >>

them stick, if you need to). Repeat with the second band. Wrap the rolls in plastic and chill until they firm up, at least an hour in the refrigerator or 30 minutes in the freezer.

4 When you're ready to bake, heat the oven to 425°F and line two baking sheets with parchment paper or a silicone baking mat (or use nonstick baking sheets). With a very sharp knife, slice each roll into 12 pieces, arrange them on a sheet at least 1 inch apart, and bake until the pastry is nicely browned and flaky (break one apart to be sure it's not still doughy in the center), and the cheese is melted but not burned, 10 to 12 minutes. If your oven doesn't heat evenly, swap the pans' positions halfway through cooking. Transfer the palmiers to a cooling rack. Serve just slightly warm or within the hour, if possible.

------------ **DO AHEAD** ------------

You can assemble the rolls to the point just before slicing and freeze them for up to one month. To refresh any leftovers, reheat them in a 350°F oven for 5 to 7 minutes.

SHANNON'S smoked salmon canapés
WITH LEMON, HORSERADISH, AND DILL

Sometimes a classic canapé is exactly the right thing to serve with drinks—light and elegant, but yummy enough to get the party started deliciously. Shannon Wheeler, who helped me so ably with this book, developed these pretty hors d'oeuvres using our local wild Oregon salmon, of course. We prefer using hot-smoked salmon, which crumbles well and has a more pronounced smoky flavor than a cold-smoked, lox-style salmon, but you could use lox in a pinch as long as you chop it fine.

-------------------- MAKES **25** CANAPÉS --------------------

1 Put the salmon into a small bowl and gently stir together with the crème fraîche, horseradish, chopped dill, lemon zest, salt, and pepper. Chill for at least 30 minutes and up to an hour to allow the flavors to blend and the texture to firm up. The longer the filling sits, however, the milder the horseradish flavor becomes, so taste and add more if needed.

2 Heat the oven to 400°F. Lay the pastry sheet on a lightly floured counter, and roll just to smooth it out into a 10-inch square. Using a 2-inch cutter, stamp out about 25 rounds of puff pastry. Arrange the rounds on a baking sheet, and bake in the hot oven until rich golden brown, about 20 minutes. Transfer to a rack to cool. Using your index finger, lightly press down the center of the puffed disks to create a well in the center.

3 Put the chilled salmon mixture in a pastry bag fitted with a large plain tip or in a heavy-duty zip-top bag with about ½ inch snipped off one corner. Pipe the filling into each puff. Garnish each top with a few capers and a small sprig of dill. Serve immediately.

4 ounces **hot-smoked salmon**, skin removed, and broken into very small flakes

1 cup **crème fraîche**

2½ tablespoons **prepared horseradish** (from a jar), plus more to taste

1 tablespoon chopped **fresh dill**, plus 25 tiny sprigs for garnish

2½ teaspoons finely grated **lemon zest**

¼ teaspoon **kosher salt**

⅛ teaspoon freshly **ground pepper**

1 sheet (about 9 ounces) **frozen puff pastry**, thawed

About 1½ tablespoons **capers** for garnish

39

ham "biscuits"

WITH HONEY-MUSTARD CRÈME FRAÎCHE

1 sheet (about 9 ounces) **frozen puff pastry**, thawed

½ cup **crème fraîche**

2 teaspoons **whole-grain mustard**

1 teaspoon **honey**

1 teaspoon **fresh lemon juice**

½ teaspoon **Worcestershire sauce**

¼ teaspoon **kosher salt**

⅛ teaspoon **cayenne pepper**

5 ounces **good-quality ham**, cut very thinly or shaved

---------- **DO AHEAD** ----------

You can make honey-mustard crème fraîche the day before, and the puffs a few hours ahead, but for the best texture, don't assemble the hors d'oeuvres until a few minutes before serving.

For this light and elegant riff on Southern ham biscuits, Smithfield-style ham, which is fairly dry and salty-sweet, would be my first choice. But it's not that easy to come by unless you live in the South. You could also use Spanish serrano ham or even good Black Forest deli ham. Whichever kind you choose, be sure to get it sliced super thin, or the biscuits will be hard to eat.

------------ MAKES ABOUT **42** BISCUITS ------------

1 Heat the oven to 400°F. On a lightly floured counter, roll the pastry into an 11-inch square. With a 1½-inch pastry cutter, stamp out about 42 rounds. Arrange the rounds on a baking sheet and bake until puffed and golden, 18 to 20 minutes. Let cool until ready to serve.

2 Meanwhile, in a small bowl, mix the crème fraîche with the mustard, honey, lemon juice, Worcestershire, salt, and cayenne. Chill a few minutes to thicken and blend the flavors.

3 To assemble the biscuits, split each pastry in half, spoon or pipe a dollop of the honey-mustard crème fraîche on the base, arrange some ham on the crème, and put on the top. Serve immediately.

MELT-IN-YOUR-MOUTH
spicy parmesan puffs

OK, we all know that there's nothing new under the culinary sun, but in this case I think I've truly invented something original: deep-fried puff pastry. The idea had been lurking in my brain for months as I loaded batch after batch of pastry into the oven for this book. "What if?" I kept asking, until I tried it on a lark and the result, to quote my twelve-year-old daughter, rocked my world: impossibly light, with a crunch more delicate than the baked version, and just a few moist layers on the inside. This is the first of several fried puff pastry recipes in this book, and I urge you to try them all.

If you're not experienced with deep-frying, you need to know two things: keep your focus because hot fat can be dangerous, and get a frying thermometer so you can keep the oil temperature steady. It's possible to make these without a thermometer, but you'll need to do more tests. To discard the used oil, let it cool completely, then funnel it back into the original bottle—if empty—or put it in a heavy-duty zip-top bag before throwing it out. Or, put it in the gas tank of your biodiesel car!

1 sheet (about 9 ounces) **frozen puff pastry**, thawed

2 cups (4 ounces) freshly and finely grated **Parmesan cheese**

¼ to ½ teaspoon ground *piment d'Espelette* or other good **ground red pepper** (cayenne is fine, so start with the smaller amount)

1 teaspoon **kosher salt**

1 to 2 quarts (depending on the size of your pan) **canola, peanut,** or **other neutral oil** for frying

-------------------- MAKES **36** PUFFS --------------------

1 On a lightly floured counter, roll the sheet of pastry just enough to smooth it out to about a 10-inch square. Cut the pastry into 6 even strips and cut each strip into 6 even pieces, to yield 36 squares. Lay several sheets of paper towels on a plate or tray. Toss the Parmesan, red pepper, and salt together in a medium bowl and spread on a plate. Arrange these near your cooktop so you can move quickly from the hot oil to the towels to the cheese.

CONTINUED >>

2 Pour the oil into a large (at least 4 quarts), heavy-based saucepan to a depth of about 1½ inches. Heat to 400°F, using a deep-frying or candy thermometer to monitor the heat. Test the temperature with one piece of pastry: Gently drop it into the oil and fry, flipping constantly using tongs or a fork, until the pastry is very puffed and golden brown, about 2 minutes. With a spider or slotted spoon, transfer to the towels for a quick blot, then drop into the cheese and roll around to coat. (Be careful, the puff will be quite hot.) When it's cool enough to handle, taste it to be sure the inside is cooked enough—it should be moist but very airy and not doughy inside.

3 Continue with the rest of the pastry, cooking about 5 at a time. Be sure to keep the oil temperature as even as possible. Move the pan off the heat if you need to cool it down a bit.

4 Serve the puffs as soon as you can; they'll stay delicious for up to 2 hours.

martini straws

I'm not a big cocktail person, but I am devoted to the classic gin martini (up, very dry, with olives, please). As I've learned more about how gin is made, I've been intrigued by the idea of using some of its key flavorings in food to serve with the cocktail. These deep-fried cheese straws are coated in a salty-zesty mixture of aged Gouda (which shares a homeland with gin's ancestor, Dutch *genever*) and lemon zest, caraway, and coriander—aromatic ingredients often found in London-style dry gin. The frying goes quickly, so be sure to set up your work area properly . . . and I'd suggest not shaking the martinis until after you're done cooking.

MAKES **40** FIVE-INCH STRAWS

1 On a lightly floured counter, roll the pastry just to smooth it out into a 10-inch square. Cut it into 2 long strips, about 5 inches wide, then cut each strip crosswise into 20 half-inch pieces to make 40 five-inch straws.

2 Lay several sheets of paper towels on a plate or tray. Toss the Gouda with the caraway, lemon zest, coriander, and salt in a small bowl and spread on a plate (make sure the lemon zest isn't clumped together). Arrange these near your cooktop so you can move quickly from the hot oil to the towels to the cheese.

3 Pour oil into a large (at least 4 quarts), heavy-based pan to a depth of about 1½ inches. Heat it to 400°F, using a deep-frying or candy thermometer to monitor the heat. Test the temperature with one piece of pastry: Gently drop it into the oil and fry, flipping constantly using tongs or a fork, until the pastry is very puffed and a deep golden, about

1 sheet (about 9 ounces) **frozen puff pastry**, thawed

2 cups (4 ounces) finely and freshly grated **aged Gouda** (4-year-old is best, but younger will work, though it's harder to grate and toss)

2 tablespoons **whole caraway seeds**, lightly toasted for 3 minutes in a dry skillet and crushed in a mortar and pestle or with a heavy pan

2 teaspoons finely grated **lemon zest** (from about 1 large lemon)

1 teaspoon **ground coriander**

1 teaspoon **kosher salt**

1 to 2 quarts (depending on the size of your pan) **canola, peanut,** or **other neutral oil** for frying

CONTINUED >>

43

2 minutes. With a spider or slotted spoon, transfer to the towels for a quick blot, then drop into the cheese and roll to coat. (Be careful, the straw will be quite hot.) When it's cool enough to handle, taste it to be sure the inside is cooked enough—it should be moist but very airy and not doughy inside.

4 Continue with the rest of the pastry, cooking about 5 at a time. Be sure to keep the oil temperature as even as possible. Move the pan off the heat if you need to cool it down a bit.

5 Serve the straws as soon as you can; they'll stay delicious for up to 2 hours.

arugula, feta, and cilantro triangles

The inspiration for these appetizers came from Greek *spanakopita*, which are tasty but just a little boring. This version gets some attitude from spicy arugula instead of spinach (though spinach is fine if you prefer), a mix of cilantro (which I could live on), and fresh mint. The better the feta, the better the triangles will be. I love the sweetness of sheep's-milk feta, such as the French Valbreso, but anything high quality will be fine.

-------------------- MAKES **28** TRIANGLES --------------------

1 Heat the oil in a large (10-inch or larger) skillet over medium-high heat. Add the shallots and a pinch of salt and sauté lightly until soft and fragrant but not browned, about 1 minute. Add the garlic, cook for 30 seconds, then add the arugula and cook, tossing frequently with tongs, until wilted and tender, about 3 minutes more. If there's a lot of moisture left in the greens, squeeze them with the back of a spoon to release as much as possible and drain it off. Chop and transfer to a bowl.

2 Fold in the cilantro, mint, feta, pine nuts, lemon zest, and pepper flakes. Taste and add more salt or pepper flakes, if necessary, to make a lively, savory filling. Refrigerate until cool.

3 On a lightly floured counter, roll the pastry into a 12-by-21-inch rectangle. Prick it all over with a fork at ½-inch intervals. Cut the rectangle into four 3-by-21-inch strips, then cut each strip into 7 squares, to yield 28 three-inch squares.

1 tablespoon **olive oil**

2 tablespoons minced **shallot**

Kosher salt

2 medium cloves **garlic**, minced

5 ounces **arugula** or **baby spinach leaves**, large stems removed, roughly chopped, rinsed well, and excess water shaken off

½ cup roughly chopped **fresh cilantro leaves**

¼ cup chopped **fresh mint leaves**

1 cup (4 ounces) crumbled **feta cheese**

¼ cup **pine nuts**, lightly toasted in a 350°F oven, then chopped

1 teaspoon finely grated **lemon zest**

Pinch of **Aleppo pepper flakes** or **cayenne pepper**

1 sheet (about 9 ounces) **frozen puff pastry**, thawed

3 tablespoons **unsalted butter**, melted

CONTINUED >>

4 With your finger and a little bowl of water, moisten two adjacent edges of a square, put a rounded teaspoon of filling in the center, fold over to make a triangle, and carefully pinch the edges to seal tightly. Repeat with the remaining pastry and filling. Brush each triangle with some melted butter, cut a couple of tiny steam vents in the top, arrange on one or two baking sheets, and chill for about 15 minutes. Heat the oven to 400°F.

5 Bake until puffed and golden brown on top and bottom, about 20 minutes. Serve immediately.

DO AHEAD

You can make the triangles and keep them in the fridge for up to one day before baking, or freeze them, unbaked, for up to one month. Bake them directly from the freezer and add a few more minutes to the cooking time.

pancetta, parmesan, and pepper quiches

These are killer for entertaining because you can assemble them ahead and freeze them. (I stole this idea from a recipe by Kate Hays published in *Fine Cooking* magazine. Thanks, Kate!) You fill your tartlets, freeze the unbaked quiches in the mini muffin tin, pop out the frozen "pucks" of quiche, and pile them into a freezer bag. When you're ready to serve, just drop the pucks back into the mini muffin tin or a tartlet pan and bake. My muffin tin has 18 cups that are 2 inches across and hold 1 ounce. You could use a different size, but if your cups are larger, you'll get fewer quiches and will need to increase the cooking time a bit. I love using pancetta, but regular smoked bacon would be fine.

------------------- MAKES **36** MINI QUICHES -------------------

1 In a medium skillet, heat the oil over medium heat; add the pancetta, and cook, stirring, until most of the fat has rendered and the pieces are browned, 6 to 10 minutes, depending on the thickness of your slices. Scoop out with a slotted spoon and drain on paper towels.

2 Drain off all but about 1 tablespoon of the fat, add the red bell pepper and a pinch of salt and cook, stirring occasionally, until fragrant, soft, and browned around the edges, 8 to 10 minutes. Add the jalapeño and continue cooking until all the peppers are completely tender, for another 2 minutes. Let cool slightly. In a medium bowl, whisk together the eggs and cream, then stir in the cooked peppers, Parmesan, Cheddar, and cooked pancetta. Season with the ½ teaspoon salt and the cayenne.

1 tablespoon **olive oil**

¼ pound thinly sliced **pancetta**, cut into ¼-inch dice

1 small **red bell pepper**, cored, seeded, and cut into ¼-inch dice (about 1 cup)

½ teaspoon **Kosher salt**, plus more to taste

2 tablespoons finely chopped and seeded **jalapeño** or **other fresh, medium-hot green chile**

3 **large eggs**

¾ cup **heavy cream** or **crème fraîche**

1 cup (2 ounces) freshly and finely grated **Parmesan cheese**

1 cup (3 ounces) freshly shredded **extra-sharp Cheddar cheese**

⅛ teaspoon **cayenne pepper** or other ground red pepper such as **piment d'Espelette**

2 sheets (about 9 ounces each) **frozen puff pastry**, thawed

CONTINUED >>

3 Heat the oven to 400°F. Lightly grease the insides of two or three mini muffin tins or bake in batches (depending on how many cups yours have). On a lightly floured counter, roll one sheet of pastry into a 10-by-18-inch rectangle. With a 3-inch pastry cutter, stamp out 18 rounds. Press the rounds into the muffin cups, and fill each one completely with about 1 tablespoon filling. Repeat with the second sheet of pastry and the remaining filling (save the scraps for another use or discard). Bake until the filling is puffed and golden and the crust is a rich golden brown, about 17 to 20 minutes. Let the quiches cool a few minutes for the best flavor; they should lift out of the muffin tin easily.

----------- **DO AHEAD** -----------

Freeze the *unbaked* quiches in the muffin tin until completely firm, two to three hours. Pop them out of the pan and put them in an airtight container or freezer bag. Freeze for up to one month. To cook, put the frozen quiches back into the muffin tin and bake at 400°F for 20 to 25 minutes.

smoky-sweet chorizo pockets
WITH DATES, BACON, AND PIQUILLO PEPPERS

2 ounces **smoked bacon** (about 3 thin or 2 thick-cut slices), chopped

2 tablespoons **olive oil**

½ cup finely chopped **onion** (about ½ a medium onion)

Kosher salt

3 tablespoons minced **garlic** (about 3 large cloves)

1 teaspoon **smoked paprika** (*pimentón de la Vera*)

¼ teaspoon **ground cumin**

⅛ teaspoon **crushed red pepper flakes**

½ cup chopped **fresh tomatoes**

1½ cups finely diced (⅛ inch) **Spanish chorizo** (about 5 ounces), mild or spicy

½ cup finely diced (⅛ inch) **piquillo peppers** (about 6 medium) or **roasted red bell peppers**

5 **Medjool dates**, pitted and finely diced

2 teaspoons **pomegranate molasses** or 1 teaspoon **balsamic vinegar**

Hot sauce to taste

½ cup chopped **fresh cilantro**

2 sheets (about 9 ounces each) **frozen puff pastry**, thawed

This savory bite was inspired by an amazing first course I had at Avec restaurant in Chicago: chorizo-stuffed dates baked in tomato-pepper sauce and served in a little cast-iron skillet. Here, I capture the excitement of that dish and wrap it up in a savory puff. It's important to use real Spanish chorizo, such as Palacios brand, not Mexican or bulk uncooked sausage. The Spanish stuff, made from pork, paprika and garlic, is smoked and ready to eat. Piquillo peppers are medium, heart-shaped roasted red peppers from Spain. And pomegranate molasses is concentrated pomegranate juice, which adds a tangy-sweet note to the filling. You can buy these ingredients at many specialty foods stores or from an online source such as *www.latienda.com*.

-------------------- MAKES **48** POCKETS --------------------

1 Cook the bacon in a large skillet over medium heat, stirring frequently, until crisp and most of the fat is rendered. With a slotted spoon, scoop the bacon bits onto a paper towel to drain. Discard the fat in the pan. Put the pan back on the heat, add the olive oil and onion; season with a little salt. Cook until soft and fragrant, about 3 minutes. Add the garlic and cook for another 30 seconds, then add the paprika, cumin, and red pepper flakes, and stir to cook the spices for a few seconds.

2 Raise the heat to medium-high, add the tomatoes, and cook until they break up a bit, 3 to 4 minutes, then add the chorizo, piquillo peppers, dates, and the cooked bacon. Cook a few minutes, stirring, to blend the flavors. Stir in the pomegranate molasses then taste and add hot sauce or salt as you like. The filling should be highly seasoned. Let cool for a few minutes, then fold in the cilantro.

50

3 Heat the oven to 425°F. On a lightly floured counter, roll one of the pastry sheets into a 10-by-15-inch rectangle. Prick the dough all over, and then cut it into four 2½-by-15-inch strips. Cut each strip into 6 equal pieces, to yield twenty-four 2½-inch squares.

4 Lay about 6 squares on the work surface. Dab each corner of each square with water. Put a rounded teaspoon of the filling in the center of each square and bring all 4 corners up to the center. Pinch tightly to fuse just the points together. Repeat with remaining squares and the second sheet of pastry.

5 Arrange the pockets on a baking sheet and chill for about 15 minutes. Bake until they're puffed and deep golden brown on the sides and bottom, and the pastry is no longer doughy, 15 to 16 minutes. Let cool on a rack for a few minutes. Serve warm.

------------ **DO AHEAD** ------------

You can make and freeze the unbaked pockets for up to one month, or refrigerate for up to four hours ahead of time. You can also completely bake them a few hours ahead and reheat briefly just before serving, but they're not quite as good as just-baked.

spiced samosa puffs
WITH CILANTRO-CHILE DIPPING SAUCE

1½ pounds **Yukon gold** or **russet potatoes**, peeled and cut into ½-inch dice

3 tablespoons **olive oil**

1 cup finely chopped **onion** (about 1 medium onion)

Kosher salt

2 to 4 tablespoons minced **fresh chile**, such as **jalapeño**

2 tablespoons minced **fresh ginger** (from one 2-inch piece)

1 tablespoon **garam masala**

2 tablespoons **unsalted butter**

1 cup **fresh** or **frozen peas** (no need to thaw)

Juice of half a **lime** or **lemon**, plus more to taste

Freshly ground **pepper** to taste

½ cup chopped **fresh cilantro**

2 sheets (about 9 ounces each) **frozen puff pastry**, thawed

Cilantro-Chile Dipping Sauce (optional; recipe follows)

I love the heady mix of flavors in Indian samosas: fragrant spices, earthy vegetables, ginger, chile, cilantro. But making the little fried turnovers from scratch is time-consuming. Tucking samosa filling into a flaky pouch of puff pastry, however, is equally delicious and so much easier. If you happen to cook with ghee (Indian clarified butter), use it, otherwise, mild olive oil is fine. Many Indian cooks make their own garam masala, but for this recipe, a premixed spice blend, such as McCormick's, is fine. I love to dip the puffs in a fragrant cilantro chutney, which is typically a purée of cilantro, chiles, and ginger mixed with yogurt. If you don't have time to make the Cilantro-Chile Dipping Sauce, you can try one from a jar, adding a bit of chopped fresh cilantro to enhance it.

---------------------- MAKES **36** SAMOSAS ----------------------

1 Put the potatoes in a pot of generously salted water, bring to a boil, and cook until very tender, about 10 minutes. Scoop out about a cup of the potato water, then drain the potatoes.

2 Meanwhile, heat the oil in a large skillet over medium-high heat; add the onion, season with salt, and cook until very soft and slightly golden, about 3 minutes. Add the chile, cook for another minute, then add the ginger and garam masala and cook until the mixture is fragrant, another minute or so.

3 Dump the drained potatoes into the pan along with the butter. With a rubber spatula, fold to blend (it's fine if the potatoes get a bit mushy), adding enough of the reserved potato water to make the mixture a bit creamy, then add the peas and lime juice. Fold until well blended. Taste and season generously with more salt and some pepper. Let cool slightly, then fold in the cilantro.

CONTINUED >>

4 Heat the oven to 400°F and line two baking sheets with parchment paper or silicone baking mats (you'll probably need to bake these in batches if baking all 36 in one session).

5 On a lightly floured counter, roll a sheet of pastry into a 14-inch square. Cut it into thirds lengthwise and thirds crosswise to make 9 squares. Roll one square to enlarge it to about 5 by 5 inches and cut in half to make two triangles. With a triangle in front of you at a right angle, spoon about 1 tablespoon filling onto the pastry just to the lower right of center. Moisten the edges of the pastry with water. Bring the top corner to the bottom corner to create a smaller triangle and pinch all around to seal tightly. Repeat with the remaining squares and the second sheet of pastry.

6 Arrange the samosas on the baking sheets and bake until lightly puffed and rich golden brown, 18 to 20 minutes. Let cool for a few minutes on a rack, then serve hot, with or without the Cilantro-Chile Dipping Sauce.

CILANTRO-CHILE DIPPING SAUCE

⅓ cup **plain yogurt**

1 tablespoon **minced onion** or **shallot**

½ teaspoon minced **fresh ginger**

1 to 2 **jalapeños**, cored, seeded, and roughly chopped

1 teaspoon **kosher salt**

1 teaspoon **sugar**

1 cup lightly packed **fresh mint leaves**

2 cups lightly packed **fresh cilantro leaves**

This sauce, which is based on a cilantro chutney from Indian food expert Julie Sahni, is so good I could put it on everything. I think there's a special affinity for potatoes, so make a double batch and keep some to dress up plain steamed potatoes, a potato frittata, or even to drizzle on mashed potatoes.

--------------------- MAKES ABOUT **1** CUP ---------------------

1 Put everything in a food processor and process until creamy. Taste and adjust seasoning. Chill for at least 30 minutes to let the flavors blend.

spicy beef and chipotle picadillo empanadas

I love meat pies of all stripes, and this Mexican-inspired version is a degree more exciting than most. The picadillo filling, which shows up in empanadas, stuffed chiles, and other Mexican dishes, is lively with the interplay of sweet raisins, tangy green olives, and smoky chipotle powder (chipotles are smoked, dried jalapeños). McCormick makes a chipotle powder now, but if you can't find it, mince about a half of a small chipotle in adobo sauce, which you'll find in a small can in the Hispanic food section of the grocery store; add more to taste because they can be very hot.

MAKES **36** THREE-INCH TURNOVERS,
OR **12** FIVE-INCH TURNOVERS

1 In a large skillet, heat the oil over medium heat. Add the onion and cook, stirring, until soft and fragrant, 3 to 4 minutes. Add the garlic and stir for a minute, then stir in the salt, chipotle, cumin, cinnamon, thyme, and oregano. Cook for about 30 seconds until very fragrant. Add the beef and cook, breaking up the chunks with your spatula, until most of the pink is gone, about 2 minutes. Add the tomato, raise the heat to medium-high, and cook, stirring, until the mixture has thickened slightly and is nicely blended, another 2 minutes. Stir in the raisins and olives. Taste and add more salt or other spices if needed. Refrigerate until cold, about one hour.

2 When the filling is cold, heat the oven to 400°F. On a lightly floured counter, roll out one sheet of pastry into a 9½-by-18-inch rectangle.

CONTINUED >>

1 tablespoon **olive oil**

¾ cup finely chopped **onion** (from 1 small onion)

2 to 3 medium cloves **garlic**, minced

1½ teaspoons **kosher salt**

1 teaspoon **chipotle powder**, plus more to taste

1 tablespoon **ground cumin**

¼ teaspoon **ground cinnamon**

1 teaspoon chopped **fresh thyme** or ½ teaspoon **dried thyme leaves** (not ground)

1 teaspoon chopped **fresh oregano** or ½ teaspoon **dried oregano leaves** (not ground)

½ pound **ground beef** (not too lean; 80% is good)

1 cup drained and chopped **canned tomato**, or seeded and chopped **fresh tomato** (about 2 medium)

¼ cup roughly chopped **raisins**

½ cup chopped **pimiento-stuffed olives**

2 sheets (about 9 ounces each) **frozen puff pastry**, thawed

1 **large egg**, beaten until blended (optional, as a glaze)

55

Prick all over at ½-inch intervals. With a 3-inch pastry cutter, stamp out 18 rounds. (To make larger empanadas, roll the pastry to a 10-by-15-inch rectangle and stamp out six 5-inch rounds.)

3 Moisten the edge of a pastry round with water. Spoon about 1 rounded measuring teaspoon of filling in the center, fold over, and press firmly to seal. Crimp the edges by pressing all around with the back of a fork. Repeat with the remaining rounds and the second sheet of pastry. Arrange the empanadas on baking sheets. With a sharp knife, cut small slits in the top of each one to release steam. Brush with the beaten egg, if using, and chill for 15 minutes in the refrigerator.

4 Bake until slightly puffed and a rich golden brown, 15 to 20 minutes. Let cool for a few minutes on a rack, then serve immediately.

savory roasted tomato tart

During the summer, my husband and I roast crates and crates of tomatoes that we get from our farmers' market. Most of them get portioned into freezer bags, to be meted out over the course of the bleak Oregon winter. The sweet, zingy tomatoes are the culinary equivalents of the "sun breaks" that shine through our rainy days, when we're lucky. But some tomatoes get set aside for these tarts, which we eat plain or garnished with whatever accents I find in the fridge: chopped briny olives, meaty-sweet anchovies, or shaved imported Parmesan or manchego cheese. Because tomato roasting takes such a long time, you might as well do a double or triple batch; they freeze really well. You can use thawed roasted tomatoes to make another tart, or use them in soups, stews, or vegetable dishes.

SERVES **8** TO **10** AS AN APPETIZER OR
3 TO **4** AS A LIGHT MAIN COURSE

1 Heat the oven to 350°F. Line a rimmed baking sheet with parchment paper or a silicone baking mat. Cut out the tomato stems, cut the tomatoes in half (lengthwise for the Romas, crosswise along the equator for round tomatoes), and arrange cut side up on the baking sheet. Drizzle with the 3 tablespoons olive oil, then sprinkle with the thyme, rosemary, and a light seasoning of salt and pepper. Roast in the oven until shrunken in size by at least half, very shriveled and browned around the edges, and concentrated in flavor. Depending on the moisture content of your tomatoes, this could take from 1½ to 3 hours. Leave to cool; they'll be less fragile and easier to handle once they're cool.

CONTINUED >>

10 large **Roma** or **other smallish round tomatoes**, such as Early Girl (2½ to 3 pounds)

3 tablespoons **extra-virgin olive oil**, plus more for brushing

1 teaspoon **fresh thyme leaves**

1 teaspoon chopped **fresh rosemary**

Kosher salt

Freshly ground **pepper**

1 sheet (about 9 ounces) **frozen puff pastry**, thawed

½ cup (2 ounces) **crumbled feta**, or 2 ounces **fresh goat cheese**, divided into small dollops

2 When the tomatoes are ready, heat the oven to 425°F and line a baking sheet with parchment paper or a silicone baking mat. On a lightly floured counter, roll the pastry to a 12-by-14-inch rectangle and cut into two 6-by-14-inch strips. Transfer the strips to the baking sheet (use two baking sheets if the strips are crowded). Prick each strip with a fork at half-inch intervals, leaving about a ½-inch border unpricked.

3 Bake until the pastry is light golden brown and starting to dry out, about 10 minutes. Take the baking sheet from the oven, press down any puffiness in the center of the strips, and arrange the tomatoes in an even layer (a few gaps are fine) on top. Return to the oven and continue baking until the pastry is golden brown (be sure to check the underneath also), the borders are puffed, and the tomatoes are hot, 12 to 15 minutes.

4 Take the baking sheet from the oven and slide the tarts to a cooling rack. Brush the edges with olive oil, sprinkle the cheese on the tarts, and cool for about 10 minutes, then slide onto a cutting board and cut crosswise into servings, 2 to 3 inches for an appetizer or larger for a main dish. Serve warm or at room temperature.

caramelized onion, crisp bacon, and roquefort tarts

1 tablespoon **olive oil** or **butter**

6 ounces (about 4 thin or 3 thick-cut
slices) **bacon**, cut into ½-inch pieces

2 pounds **yellow** or **sweet onions**
(about 3 large), cut into ¼-inch slices

1 teaspoon **kosher salt**

Freshly ground **pepper**

1½ teaspoons **fresh thyme leaves**

Two 4-inch sprigs **fresh rosemary**

1 sheet (about 9 ounces) **frozen
puff pastry**, thawed

4 teaspoons **Dijon mustard**

¾ cup (3 ounces) crumbled **good-quality
blue cheese**, such as Roquefort,
crumbled

Caramelizing onions is one of my joys in the kitchen, odd as that may sound, because such a small amount of work pays off so handsomely. The transformation of a harsh, crunchy raw onion into a pan full of tawny-sweet, silky compote is an object lesson on what's cool about cooking. The onions keep in the fridge for several days, so you could make a double batch and save half to pop into an omelet, fold into pilaf, or pile on top of a steak later in the week. I also love making this with pancetta, an unsmoked Italian bacon that's now available in most grocery stores, and to boost the smokiness, I use a smoked blue cheese made in Oregon by Rogue Creamery.

------------------- SERVES **14** AS AN APPETIZER -------------------
OR **4** AS A MAIN COURSE

1 Spread a double layer of paper towels on a plate. In a large skillet (12 inches), heat the oil over medium heat, add the bacon, and cook until most of the fat has rendered, but the bacon isn't super crisp (you'll cook it further in the oven, and you want it to remain tender), 7 to 10 minutes. Remove the bacon and drain it on the paper towels. Pour off all but 2 tablespoons of the bacon grease.

2 Add the onions to the pan, increase the heat to medium-high, add the salt, season generously with pepper, and toss in the thyme and rosemary. Toss the onions with tongs until they all begin to wilt a bit. Cover the pan, reduce the heat to medium-low, and sweat the onions until they're quite soft and translucent, 10 to 12 minutes. Remove the lid, increase the heat to medium-high, and continue cooking, stirring frequently, until the onions are deep golden, very sweet, and brown juices are forming on the bottom of the pan, another 10 minutes. Let cool in the pan; remove the sprigs of rosemary.

3 When the onions are cool, heat the oven to 400°F. On a lightly floured counter, roll the pastry into a 10-by-14-inch rectangle and cut into two 5-by-14-inch strips. Transfer the strips to a baking sheet (it's fine if they're closely spaced—you'll be folding up the edges). With a small offset spatula or the back of a spoon, spread the mustard down the length of the strips, leaving a ½-inch border on each of the long sides. Arrange the onions over the mustard, making sure they're in an even layer and that they come all the way to the edge of each short end. Fold up the long sides to create a ½-inch border, pressing lightly to secure it. Hold a table knife upright and tap along the border at ½-inch intervals to indent the pastry just a bit; this will crimp it and keep it from unfolding too much during cooking.

4 Bake the strips until the pastry is light brown and the borders are puffed, 15 to 17 minutes. Take the baking sheet from the oven, sprinkle the cheese and bacon over the onions, and continue cooking until the borders and underside of the pastry are deep golden brown and the cheese has started to melt, 5 to 6 minutes. Slide the pastries onto a cooling rack and let cool for about 10 minutes, then slide onto a cutting board and cut crosswise into 2-inch strips. Serve warm, but soon—the tarts get soggy if reheated.

big first
courses
AND
main
dishes

feta and dill tart
WITH LEMONY SPINACH SALAD

2 large eggs

⅓ cup **crème fraîche** or **heavy cream**

2 tablespoons chopped **fresh dill**,
plus ½ cup loosely packed **dill sprigs**
for the salad (optional)

1 teaspoon finely grated **lemon zest**

½ teaspoon **kosher salt**,
plus more for the salad

Freshly ground **pepper**

1 sheet (about 9 ounces) **frozen
puff pastry**, thawed

1 cup (about 4 ounces) crumbled
good-quality feta

---

4 small handfuls **baby spinach** or
baby arugula leaves, washed
and dried well

3 tablespoons **extra-virgin olive oil**

1 tablespoon **fresh lemon juice**,
plus more to taste

I like piling the spinach salad right on top of this tart, because the cool, slightly bitter leaves contrast beautifully with the tangy, salty tart below. But for a cocktail snack, skip the salad and simply cut the tart into smaller pieces. This is not a particularly good reheater, so make it close to serving time.

SERVES **4**

1 Heat the oven to 425°F. In a medium bowl, whisk the eggs, crème fraîche, chopped dill, lemon zest, ½ teaspoon salt, and about 10 grinds of pepper.

2 On a lightly floured counter, roll the pastry into an 11-by-13-inch rectangle. Line a baking sheet with parchment paper or a silicone baking mat (in case there are any leaks), and lay the pastry on the sheet. Wet the edges with water and fold over a ¾-inch border. Distribute the feta evenly within the border, and then carefully pour the egg mixture over the cheese, taking care that it doesn't slosh onto the border. Carefully transfer the baking sheet to the oven and bake until the pastry is puffed and brown on the border and the underside, and the filling is golden brown, 18 to 20 minutes.

3 Slide the tart off the pan and onto a rack to cool a bit. Transfer to a cutting board and cut into four rectangles, so that each piece gets some border. Put the tart onto plates.

4 In a large bowl, toss the spinach and dill sprigs (if using) with the olive oil and lemon juice until evenly coated. Sprinkle with salt, pepper, and more lemon juice to taste. Arrange a handful of salad on each piece of tart and serve immediately.

garlicky sausage
WITH GRAINY MUSTARD AND HERBS in a crust

½ cup **whole-grain mustard**

1 tablespoon chopped **fresh tarragon**

1 sheet (about 9 ounces) **frozen puff pastry**, thawed

3 heaping tablespoons freshly and finely grated **Parmesan cheese**

Four 5-inch lengths **smoked kielbasa** or other **cooked garlicky sausage**

1 **large egg**, lightly beaten

Think "pigs in a blanket," but with a French accent. I like to use kielbasa, though any juicy, ready-to-eat sausage will work . . . except Vienna sausages in a can, please. A whole portion makes a terrific light dinner when served with a salad of frisée, bacon, and apples and a glass of cold dry cider. And the minis are a savory treat with cocktails. If you can't find whole-grain mustard, sometimes called *moutarde à l'ancienne*, use classic Dijon.

SERVES **4** OR MAKES **40** HORS D'OEUVRES

1 Stir together the mustard and tarragon and set aside.

2 On a lightly floured counter, roll the pastry into a 9-by-12-inch rectangle and prick the dough all over with the tines of a fork at 1-inch intervals. Cut in half lengthwise and then crosswise, to yield four 4½-by-6-inch pieces that will wrap the length of the sausage with just a bit sticking out at either end.

3 Heat the oven to 400°F. Spread 2 teaspoons of the mustard mixture across one short edge of one piece of pastry. Sprinkle with 1 teaspoon cheese. Position a sausage on the mustard, moisten the other short edge with water, wrap the sausage in the pastry and then press firmly along the moistened edge to seal. Position on baking sheet seam side down. Repeat with remaining ingredients. Reserve the remaining Parmesan and save the rest of the mustard for dipping.

4 Bake until the pastry is puffed and light brown, about 15 minutes. Pull out the baking sheet, brush the tops with egg and sprinkle with the remaining Parmesan. Continue baking until the pastry is cooked all the way through and the sausage is thoroughly heated, another 4 to 5 minutes. Serve with a spoonful of the remaining mustard and a crisp green salad.

5 TO MAKE COCKTAIL MINIS: Following the directions above, wrap the lengths of sausage so they're completely covered with pastry. Chill until firm, at least 15 minutes. With a very sharp knife, cut into ½-inch slices. Arrange on a parchment-lined baking sheet. Bake at 375°F until the pastry is puffed, about 15 minutes, skipping the egg wash and Parmesan step. Serve with the remaining mustard.

provençal pizza

This flaky-crusted "pizza" is easy to make, so serve big squares of it as dinner on nights when you're short on time. Or, for guests, serve smaller pizzas as an appetizer. If there are non-anchovy eaters at your table, you can put the anchovies only on half the tart, but they're awfully good, so I'd advise you not to skip them yourself. (Look for Ortiz brand anchovies, which are especially sweet and meaty, and not too salty.) Originally, I developed this recipe as a way to use leftover ratatouille, but the supermarket is full of other options: caponata, Greek eggplant spread (I use Peloponnese Roasted Eggplant Spread), roasted red peppers. Feel free to play with other ingredients as well—caramelized onions, grilled zucchini, fresh mozzarella—just don't overload the crust or it will get soggy.

SERVES **8** AS AN APPETIZER
OR **2** TO **3** AS A LIGHT MAIN COURSE

1 Heat the oven to 400°F. On a lightly floured counter, roll the pastry into an 11-by-15-inch rectangle. Slide it onto a baking sheet and prick all over with a fork. Moisten the perimeter with a little water and fold up the edge to create a ½-inch border.

2 Spread the ratatouille evenly over the pastry. Distribute the tomatoes, feta, olives, and sun-dried tomatoes on top. Bake for about 18 minutes, then arrange the anchovies in a neat pattern on top and sprinkle with the Parmesan. Continue baking until the pastry is puffed around the edges and golden brown (check the underside, too), another 4 to 5 minutes. Slide onto a cutting board, immediately brush the edges with some olive oil (if using), and sprinkle with the basil. Cut into squares and serve slightly warm.

1 sheet (about 9 ounces) **frozen puff pastry**, thawed

¾ cup **ratatouille, caponata,** or other Mediterranean vegetable condiment (drained if very juicy)

½ cup halved **grape** or other small tomatoes

⅓ cup crumbled **feta cheese**

⅓ cup roughly chopped pitted **kalamata, niçoise,** or other good-quality black olives

Scant ¼ cup chopped **sun-dried tomatoes in oil**, drained

8 **anchovy fillets**

½ cup (about 1 ounce) freshly and finely grated **Parmesan cheese**

Olive oil, for brushing (optional)

2 tablespoons roughly chopped **fresh basil or parsley leaves**

IVY'S swiss chard and goat cheese tart

2 tablespoons **extra-virgin olive oil**

1 cup finely chopped **onion**
(about 1 medium onion,
preferably a sweet variety)

1 tablespoon minced **garlic**

1 large bunch **Swiss chard**, stems
and ribs removed, roughly chopped
(6 cups loosely packed)

Kosher salt

Freshly ground **pepper**

1 sheet (about 9 ounces) **frozen
puff pastry**, thawed

4 ounces **fresh mozzarella**,
very thinly sliced

1 ounce **aged goat cheese** (preferably a
smoked version), cut into small pieces

2 tablespoons **pine nuts**, lightly toasted
in a 350°F oven for 3 to 5 minutes

1 teaspoon **truffle oil** (optional)

The tart is the creation of Ivy Manning, the talented and beautiful Portland chef who helped me test the recipes in this book. Ivy has a way with vegetables, and this recipe is tasty proof of that. She likes to use Swiss chard, but in the cold months you could try a heartier green such as Tuscan kale (a.k.a. black kale, dinosaur kale, or cavolo nero); it will need to sauté a few minutes more to get tender.

------------------   SERVES **8** AS AN APPETIZER   ------------------
OR **4** AS A LIGHT MAIN COURSE

1 Heat the oven to 400°F. In a large skillet, heat the oil over medium heat and sauté the onion until soft, golden, and fragrant but not browned, about 8 minutes. Add the garlic and sauté for another minute. Add the chard leaves, season generously with salt and pepper to taste, and sauté, tossing with tongs until wilted and tender, about 5 minutes.

2 Line a baking sheet with parchment paper or a silicone baking mat. On a lightly floured counter, roll the pastry into an 11-by-15-inch rectangle. Slide the pastry onto the baking sheet and prick all over with a fork. Moisten the perimeter with a little water and fold up the edge to create a 1-inch border.

3 Arrange the mozzarella slices evenly over the pastry, distribute the chard, and top with the goat cheese and pine nuts. Bake until the pastry is puffed around the edges and golden brown (check the underside, too), 22 to 25 minutes. Slide onto a cutting board, drizzle with the truffle oil (if using), and cut into squares. Serve slightly warm.

melted leek tart

WITH FENNEL SAUSAGE AND GOAT CHEESE

Once you taste the cooked leeks, you'll understand why I call them "melted"—slow cooking makes the texture so satiny and brings out the leeks' intense sweetness. Be vigilant when washing them, because sometimes there's a remarkable amount of grit hiding between the layers, especially right where the dark green part merges with the white. If you can find a sausage that's already strongly fennel-scented, you can omit the additional fennel seed.

SERVES **12** AS AN APPETIZER
OR **6** AS A MAIN COURSE

1 Trim the roots and dark green end from the leeks, leaving just the white and very light green parts. Split the leeks in half lengthwise and rinse well, separating the layers to get any grit nestled between. Cut crosswise into ¼-inch slices. Set aside.

2 Heat a large skillet over medium-low heat, add 1 tablespoon of the oil, the sausage, and the fennel seeds, breaking the meat into small chunks with a wooden spoon. Cook slowly until no longer pink, 7 to 9 minutes, taking care not to brown the sausage. Scoop it out with a slotted spoon and drain on paper towels. Pour off any grease from the pan, but don't wash it.

3 Add the remaining 3 tablespoons olive oil to the pan, increase the heat to medium, and add the leeks, rosemary sprig, and salt. Cover the pan (use foil if your skillet doesn't have a lid) and cook, stirring and scraping the bottom of the pan often so the juices don't burn, until the

3½ pounds **leeks** (about 5 medium)

¼ cup **olive oil**

8 ounces **bulk mild Italian sausage**

1 teaspoon **whole fennel seeds**, crushed

One 5-inch sprig **fresh rosemary**
or **thyme**

1 teaspoon **kosher salt**

2 sheets (about 9 ounces each) **frozen puff pastry**, thawed

5 ounces **fresh goat cheese**

½ cup (1 ounce) freshly and finely grated **Parmesan cheese**

CONTINUED >>

leeks are just tender, about 10 minutes. Remove the lid and continue cooking until the leeks are very tender and the juices are just barely browning on the bottom of the pan, another 3 to 5 minutes. If the leeks seem like they're going to burn or stick at any time, add a few spoonfuls of water to loosen. Set aside to cool and remove the rosemary sprig.

4 Heat the oven to 400°F. On a lightly floured counter, roll one sheet of the pastry into an 11-by-15-inch rectangle. Slide it onto a baking sheet and prick all over with a fork. Moisten the perimeter with a little water and fold up the edge to create a ½-inch border. Press firmly to secure the border.

5 Spread half of the leeks evenly over the pastry. Distribute half of the sausage and goat cheese (spooned into small dollops for even coverage) on top, and sprinkle with ¼ cup of the Parmesan. Repeat with the other sheet of pastry and remaining ingredients. Bake until the pastry is puffed around the edges and golden brown (check the underside, too), 22 to 25 minutes. Slide the tarts onto a rack to cool, then onto a cutting board. Cut into squares and serve slightly warm.

MY ULTIMATE comfort creamed tuna

Yes, this dish is one step away from tuna casserole, but that one step makes all the difference. This version has all the comfort appeal of that childhood classic, but with a touch of sophistication for a grown-up palate. The flavor gets updated with lemon zest and Parmesan cheese, and instead of potato-chip topping, this dish gets its crunch from a simple sandwich of puff pastry. I tend to use chunk light tuna in oil because it's flavorful and tender (and because this darker tuna generally comes from smaller fish with lower levels of mercury).

------------------------------ SERVES **2** ------------------------------

1 Heat the oven to 400°F. On a lightly floured counter, roll the dough lightly just to smooth it, then cut it into two pieces, each about 3 by 4½ inches. Put the pastry on a small baking sheet and bake in the hot oven until puffed and nicely golden brown, 20 minutes.

2 Meanwhile, in a small, heavy-based saucepan, melt the butter over medium heat. Add the flour and whisk until smooth, then whisk for about 30 seconds. Add the milk, whisk vigorously until the sauce is smooth, then reduce the heat to low and cook, whisking often, another 2 to 3 minutes to cook off the floury taste. Season generously with salt and pepper. Gently fold in the tuna and Parmesan. Add the lemon zest and juice and taste for seasoning, adding more salt, pepper, or lemon juice to taste. The tuna should be creamy and loose, but not runny. Add a little more milk, and reheat gently, if necessary.

3 Split the pastries in half horizontally, with your knife parallel to the work surface, as though you're splitting open a sandwich roll, and put the bottoms on two small plates. Spoon the creamed tuna on the base, then cover with the top. Serve immediately.

One 3-by-9-inch piece **frozen puff pastry**, thawed (about ⅓ sheet, or 3 ounces)

1 tablespoon **unsalted butter**

1 tablespoon **all-purpose flour**

½ cup **milk**, plus more if needed

Kosher salt

Freshly ground **pepper**

Two 6-ounce cans **chunk light tuna in oil**, drained

2 tablespoons freshly and finely grated **Parmesan cheese**

1 teaspoon finely grated **lemon zest**

2 teaspoons **fresh lemon juice**, plus more to taste

73

saffron-scented seafood tart
WITH RED PEPPER SWIRL

⅓ cup packed (2 ounces) **roasted red pepper**

2 teaspoons **smoked paprika**

1½ teaspoons **kosher salt**, divided

4 **large eggs**

1 cup plus 1 tablespoon **heavy cream**, divided

1 tablespoon **olive oil**

¾ cup finely chopped **onion** (about 1 small onion)

¾ cup cored and finely chopped **fennel**

1 large clove **garlic**, minced

¼ teaspoon crumbled **saffron threads**

½ cup (1 ounce) freshly and finely grated **Parmesan cheese**

1 teaspoon finely grated **lemon zest**

10 drops **hot sauce**, such as Tabasco

1 sheet (about 9 ounces) **frozen puff pastry**, thawed

½ pound **cooked shellfish** such as shrimp, bay shrimp, scallops, or crabmeat

1 cup **diced tomato**, set over a strainer to drain for 15 minutes

My inspiration for the flavors in this tart came from the southern French soup bouillabaisse, though my daughter, Charlotte, likes to call it "paella pie," and indeed it has a Spanish accent as well. Fragrant fennel, sweet seafood, and smoky red pepper mingle in a delicate saffron-scented custard. I like to use cooked shrimp (little bay shrimp work fine), but you could use a mix of shrimp, cooked scallops, and crabmeat if you like. For the red pepper swirl, any good-quality roasted red pepper from a jar is fine, but if you can find Spanish piquillo peppers, they'll add another layer of smoke and spice to the tart.

-------------------------- SERVES **6** TO **8** --------------------------

1 Combine the red pepper, paprika, ½ teaspoon of the salt, 1 of the eggs, and 1 tablespoon of the heavy cream in a food processor or blender and process to make a smooth purée. Refrigerate until ready to use.

2 In a medium skillet, heat the oil over medium-high heat. Add the onion, fennel, and the rest of the salt and sauté, stirring frequently, until the vegetables are soft and fragrant but not at all browned, 3 to 4 minutes. Add the garlic, cook for another 30 seconds, then add the saffron and cook for a few seconds more. Set aside to cool slightly.

3 In a large bowl, whisk the remaining 3 eggs, the rest of the cream, Parmesan, lemon zest, and hot sauce. Fold in the onion mixture. Refrigerate until ready to use.

4 Heat the oven to 375°F. On a lightly floured counter, roll the pastry into a 14-inch square, prick it all over, then lay it in an 11-inch removable-bottom tart pan. Gently press the pastry into the pan, making sure not to stretch it, pressing into the corners and up the sides. Trim the pastry so it's even with the top of the pan and freeze, uncovered, for at least 20 minutes to firm up.

5 Put a piece of parchment paper or foil over the pastry, fill with pie weights, dried beans, or rice, and bake until light brown and slightly puffed, 20 to 25 minutes. Remove the pie weights and parchment, turn the oven down to 325°F and continue cooking until the pastry is dry in the center and light golden brown, 10 to 15 minutes (this is called blind baking). If the center puffs up a lot, gently press it back down, trying not to make any holes.

6 Put the tart pan on a baking sheet for easier moving. Scatter the seafood and diced tomato evenly over the surface of the tart, give the custard another whisk, then pour it into the shell. Drizzle the reserved red pepper purée over the tart and bake until the custard is just set and the pastry is nicely browned, 25 to 35 minutes. Let cool for at least 15 minutes before cutting and serving; the tart is best just lightly warm.

artichoke, basil, and fontina tart

1 tablespoon **olive oil**

½ cup finely chopped **onion**
 (about ½ a medium onion)

1 sheet (about 9 ounces) **frozen
 puff pastry**, thawed

Butter, for the pan

3 large **eggs**

1 cup **crème fraîche** or **heavy cream**

1 cup grated **fontina** or **Havarti cheese**

½ cup (1 ounce) freshly and finely grated
 Parmesan cheese

3 tablespoons sliced **fresh basil leaves**

¼ teaspoon **kosher salt**

Pinch **cayenne**

Pinch freshly grated **nutmeg**

2 ounces **prosciutto** (about 5 thin slices),
 most of the fat removed,
 cut into ½-inch pieces

1 cup **artichoke hearts**
 (from about a 14-ounce can),
 roughly chopped or sliced

The filling in this tart isn't too deep, so in every bite there's enough crisp puffed crust to perfectly complement the creamy, salty, basil-scented custard. The tart, which is like a quiche but more sophisticated, is best about a half-hour out of the oven; giving it a brief rest makes the texture smoother. Using frozen, canned, or jarred artichokes is fine, unless you're a maniac—then use freshly steamed and trimmed. Canned and jarred artichoke hearts vary wildly in quality, though, so taste before you use. (I like Matiz brand, from Spain; they're spendy but worth the splurge.) If the marinade or brine is too strong, rinse gently and pat dry. To make this vegetarian, substitute a diced roasted red pepper for the prosciutto.

SERVES 6 TO 8

1 Heat the oil in a small skillet over medium-high heat, add the onion, and sauté until tender and fragrant, 2 to 3 minutes. Set aside.

2 On a lightly floured counter, roll the pastry into a 12-inch square. Invert a 9-inch pie plate onto the pastry and cut out a round about an inch larger than the plate; discard the scraps or save them for another use (you can refreeze them if you like). Lightly butter the inside of the pie plate and then carefully drape the pastry round into it. Tuck the overhanging pastry under itself to make a neat double edge. Prick the crust with a fork at ½-inch intervals. Chill for 30 minutes in the freezer or 1 hour in the fridge.

3 Heat the oven to 425°F. Line the chilled pastry with parchment paper or foil and fill with pie weights or dried beans or rice (fold the parchment paper toward the center so it doesn't get stuck in the pastry edge as it puffs). Bake the empty pastry shell until the edges are puffed and brown, about 20 minutes. Lower the heat to 325°F. Remove the parchment paper and weights and continue baking for another 5 to 7 minutes to dry out the center of the crust (this is called blind baking).

4 In a large bowl, whisk the eggs, crème fraîche, fontina, Parmesan, cooked onion, basil, salt, cayenne, and nutmeg.

5 Scatter the prosciutto and artichoke hearts in the tart shell, then pour in the egg mixture. Return to the oven and bake until the filling is lightly browned and just set (poke it with a knife to be sure it's no longer liquid), 35 to 45 minutes. Let cool for 20 to 30 minutes before serving, or cool to room temperature and then reheat gently in a 350°F oven.

DO AHEAD

This tart can be "refreshed" the next day; simply reheat slices on a baking sheet in a 350°F oven for about 10 minutes.

roasted chicken potpie
WITH SPRING VEGETABLES

2¼ pounds **chicken thighs** or whole **legs**

Kosher **salt**

Freshly ground **pepper**

4 cups low-sodium **chicken broth**

3 medium **carrots**, peeled and cut into
   ½-inch dice, to yield about 1 cup

12 ounces **asparagus** (about 18 spears),
   woody ends trimmed, cut into
   1-inch pieces

2 tablespoons **unsalted butter**, if needed

¼ cup **all-purpose flour**

3 tablespoons chopped mixed **fresh
   tender herbs** (I like a mix of parsley,
   dill, and chives)

½ teaspoon lightly packed finely grated
   lemon zest

Fresh lemon juice, to taste

1 sheet (about 9 ounces) **frozen
   puff pastry**, thawed

1 cup **fresh** or **frozen peas**
   (no need to thaw)

Heavy cream for brushing the pastry
   (optional)

2 tablespoons freshly and finely grated
   Parmesan cheese, for dusting the
   pastry (optional)

Though we all have fond childhood memories of frozen chicken potpie (well, I do, anyway), white-meat chicken in a pasty white sauce isn't all that appealing to grown-ups. This version brings the true rich, savory flavor of roast chicken to a potpie. I use chicken legs or thighs here because dark meat indisputably has more flavor than breast meat, and the moist texture is perfect in a sauce. I call for a mix of "spring" vegetables, but use what feels seasonal: mushrooms in fall, mixed root vegetables in winter, squash and peppers in summer. This recipe uses a neat trick to avoid the potpie pitfall of underdone pastry in the middle of the pie: cutting the pastry to the size of the dish, baking it separately until almost finished, then transferring it to the chicken stew in the potpie dish to finish cooking, which marries the crust to the sauce without sogginess.

SERVES **4** TO **6**

1 Heat the oven to 400°F. Season the chicken generously with salt and pepper and arrange in a single layer in a heavy flameproof pan, such as a large skillet or small roasting pan. Roast the chicken until tender and the juices run clear, or it registers 175°F on an instant-read thermometer, about 45 minutes. Transfer the chicken to a plate and let it cool until you can handle it easily. Pour all the fat from the pan into a small bowl. *Do not* rinse out the pan; the cooked-on juices will be part of the sauce.

2 Meanwhile, put the broth in a medium saucepan and bring it to a boil. Add the carrots and cook until just barely tender, about 3 minutes.

CONTINUED >>

78

Scoop them out with a slotted spoon and set aside. Add the asparagus to the boiling broth and cook for about 30 seconds; scoop out and add to the carrots. Set aside the vegetables and the broth.

3 When the chicken has cooled, pull off the skin (it should be nice and crisp, so enjoy a piece as a snack), cut off the meat, and cut into small pieces. Add to the vegetables.

4 Put the roasting pan over medium heat and add back about 2 tablespoons of the chicken fat (if you don't have enough, use the butter). Add the flour and whisk to make a smooth paste, called a roux. Cook the roux for about 1 minute, whisking constantly, then slowly whisk in the broth to create a smooth sauce. Cook the sauce, whisking frequently, until it's reduced to about 3 cups, is very smooth, and has the consistency of thick gravy, 10 to 15 minutes. Remove from the heat, add the herbs, lemon zest, lemon juice, and a generous amount of pepper. It will probably be plenty salty, but if not, add more salt.

5 Heat the oven to 400°F. On a lightly floured counter, roll the pastry just a bit larger than the size and shape of the top of your baking dish (at least 1½-quart capacity); you can also make this using individual oven-proof bowls or ramekins. Slide the pastry onto a baking sheet and bake until puffed and light brown, about 15 minutes. Meanwhile, fold the cooked vegetables, the peas, and chicken into the sauce, and simmer gently to heat everything through.

6 When the pastry is ready, scrape the filling into the baking dish, transfer the pastry top over the filling. If you like, brush the top with a little heavy cream and sprinkle with grated Parmesan. Return the pot-pie to the oven and continue cooking until the filling is hot and the pastry is a deep golden brown, another 3 to 4 minutes. Serve immediately.

DO AHEAD

You can prepare the chicken, vegetables and sauce one day ahead. Refrigerate the sauce separately.

chicken, fontina, and prosciutto packets
WITH DIJON-SAGE CREAM SAUCE

4 large (8- to 10-ounce) **boneless, skinless chicken breast halves**

Kosher salt

Freshly ground **pepper**

1 tablespoon **olive oil**, plus more as needed

1 tablespoon **unsalted butter**

All-purpose flour, for dredging

DIJON-SAGE CREAM SAUCE

¼ cup **cognac** or **white vermouth**

½ cup low-sodium **chicken broth**

1 cup **crème fraîche** or **heavy cream**

3 whole **fresh sage leaves**

1 tablespoon **Dijon mustard**

1 tablespoon **unsalted butter** (optional)

2 sheets (about 9 ounces each) **frozen puff pastry**, thawed

2 tablespoons **Dijon mustard**

4 ounces very thinly sliced **prosciutto** (or use a **good-quality cooked ham**, such as a Black Forest style)

------- INGREDIENTS CONTINUED -------

I've paired mild chicken breasts with the classic ingredients of an Italian saltimbocca—sage and prosciutto—but this is just a starting place. Fontina adds richness, and you could make an American version with pepper bacon (cooked) and aged Cheddar; or use mozzarella and sun-dried tomatoes for a gooier, Mediterranean-inspired version.

-------------------- SERVES **8** --------------------

1 Trim any fat from the breasts. If the tenders are attached, you can either pull them off and use for something else or just leave them on—as you pound the chicken, the tender will integrate with the rest of the meat. Lay a heavy plastic bag on the chicken and pound with a meat pounder, a heavy rolling pin, or the bottom of a small heavy pot until the chicken is an even thickness (which is important for even cooking), about ½ inch. Cut each breast in half crosswise.

2 Season each chicken piece lightly with salt and pepper. Heat the oil and butter in a large heavy skillet (preferably not nonstick) over medium-high heat. When the butter stops foaming, carefully dredge each chicken piece in flour, shake off the excess, and sauté until lightly browned but not cooked all the way through, 4 to 6 minutes total. (To avoid crowding the pan, you can cook the chicken in two batches, adding a bit more oil for the second batch.) Transfer to a plate, cover, and chill for about 30 minutes. *Do not* rinse out the pan yet.

3 TO MAKE THE DIJON-SAGE CREAM SAUCE: Pour off any extra fat from the skillet, return to medium-high heat, and add the cognac. Boil until it's reduced to a glaze, scraping to dissolve any cooked-on juices. Add the broth and boil until reduced to about 1 tablespoon, then add the crème fraîche and sage, reducing to a nice saucy consistency, then whisk in the mustard. Taste and adjust salt and pepper. Reserve until ready to reheat and serve (you'll remove the sage leaves and add the butter at the last minute).

4 Heat the oven to 400°F. On a lightly floured counter, roll one of the pastry sheets into a 14-inch square. Cut the sheet into four 7-inch squares; repeat with the second sheet.

5 Spread a little less than a teaspoon of mustard in the center of each pastry. Arrange the prosciutto on the mustard, cutting the pieces so they're about the same size as the chicken pieces; it's fine to layer more than one piece. Distribute both cheeses evenly over the prosciutto, then position the chicken on top of the cheese, pressing to snug everything together.

6 Moisten the edges of the pastry with a little water, then bring each corner to the center on top of the chicken, overlapping the edges a bit. Press firmly along the seams to make a tight package. Arrange the chicken packages on a baking sheet, seam side down.

7 Brush the surface with the egg wash, and, if you like, arrange a sage leaf on top, pressing so it sticks. Bake until the pastry is puffed and deep golden brown and the chicken is cooked through (165°F on an instant-read thermometer), 25 to 30 minutes.

8 Remove the sage leaves from the sauce and reheat it very gently, whisking in the butter if using. Drizzle some sauce on each dinner plate and arrange the chicken on top. Serve immediately.

2 cups (6 ounces) grated **fontina cheese**

1 cup (2 ounces) freshly and finely grated **Parmesan cheese**

1 **large egg**, beaten, for glazing

8 pretty **fresh sage leaves**, for decoration (optional)

MOROCCAN-SPICED chicken and almond pie

2 tablespoons **olive oil**

1½ cups finely chopped **onion**
(about 1 large onion)

3 tablespoons minced **fresh ginger**
(about one 3-inch piece)

2 tablespoons minced **garlic**
(about 4 medium cloves)

1 teaspoon **turmeric**

1 cup homemade or low-sodium
chicken broth

Small pinch **saffron** (about 10 threads)

3 tablespoons **unsalted butter**, melted

4 **large eggs**, beaten

2 cups shredded **cooked chicken**

¼ cup roughly chopped **cilantro**

¼ cup chopped **fresh parsley**

Kosher salt to taste, plus ½ teaspoon

½ cup **slivered almonds**, toasted in
a 350°F oven for 7 minutes and
ground in a food processor

2 tablespoons **powdered sugar**

1 teaspoon **ground cinnamon**

¼ teaspoon **cayenne pepper**

2 sheets (about 9 ounces each)
frozen puff pastry, thawed

Not your everyday chicken potpie, this recipe is a riff on a Moroccan *b'steeya*, that exotically spiced pastry filled with tender poultry, herbs, and spices and dusted with almonds and powdered sugar. B'steeya is usually served as a first course, but I like to eat my version for dinner with a simple salad of arugula and oranges tossed in a cumin-honey vinaigrette. To save time, I suggest using rotisserie chicken, but please try to avoid the ones that are "injected" with brine solutions to make them tender. (They're salty and spongy, like luncheon meat, not chicken.) You can cook your own chicken, too: Simmer about four medium thighs in water seasoned with onion, cilantro stems, and salt, then cool and shred.

SERVES **6** TO **8**

1 In a medium skillet, heat the oil over medium heat, add the onion and sauté, stirring, until fragrant and soft, but not brown, 3 to 4 minutes. Add the ginger and garlic and cook for another minute, then stir in the turmeric. Set aside.

2 In a medium nonstick skillet, boil the chicken broth until reduced to ¼ cup. Add the saffron and about 1 tablespoon of the butter, reduce the heat to just below a simmer, and slowly stir in the eggs. You want the eggs scrambled, but very soft, so take your time and stir constantly until the eggs are thickened, about 3 minutes; a heatproof silicone spatula works well for this. Remove from the heat and fold in the sautéed onion mixture. Carefully fold in the shredded chicken, cilantro, and parsley. Season to taste with salt. Let cool.

3 Heat the oven to 375°F. In a small bowl, mix the ground almonds with the powdered sugar, cinnamon, ½ teaspoon salt, and cayenne. On a lightly floured counter, roll out one sheet of pastry into a 12-inch square. Transfer the pastry to a 9-inch pie pan and trim with a paring knife or kitchen scissors so the pastry comes just to the outer rim of the pan. Save the scraps for decoration if you like.

4 Melt the remaining 2 tablespoons of butter and brush some of it on the bottom of the pastry. Sprinkle on 2 tablespoons of the almond mixture, then spread the chicken filling evenly in the pastry. Sprinkle on another 2 tablespoons of the almond mixture. Roll the second sheet of pastry to a 10-inch square and cut out a 10-inch round (using a plate or pot lid as a template). Moisten the rim of the pastry with water, lay the second sheet over the pie, and crimp the edges to seal well. Cut 5 small slits in a spoke pattern in the center to release steam. Cut the pastry scraps into decorative shapes, moisten the undersides with water and decorate the pie, if you like. Brush the whole surface with more melted butter.

5 Bake until the crust is deep golden brown on the top and bottom, 30 to 35 minutes. Remove from the oven, brush with the remaining butter, and sprinkle all over with the remaining almond mixture. Let cool for 10 to 15 minutes to firm up, then serve warm.

wild salmon in pastry with savory mushroom stuffing
AND LEMON-CAPER BEURRE BLANC

2 tablespoons **olive oil**

¼ cup minced **shallot** or **onion**
(about ½ a small onion)

Kosher salt

About 2 cups (12 ounces) **cremini mush-rooms** (or a mix of cremini and wild), stems trimmed, chopped very fine with a chef's knife or food processor

Freshly ground **pepper**

2 tablespoons **crème fraîche** or **heavy cream**

1 teaspoon lightly packed finely grated **lemon zest**

2 tablespoons chopped **fresh dill**

2 tablespoon **capers**, drained and roughly chopped

1 sheet (about 9 ounces) **frozen puff pastry**, thawed

1 pound **skinless center-cut salmon fillet** (preferably wild), about 1 inch thick, cut into 4 portions

1 **large egg**, beaten

3 cups loosely packed **mixed bitter salad greens**, such as arugula, tat soi, and mizuna (optional)

Lemon-Caper Beurre Blanc (recipe follows)

This recipe delivers lots of deliciousness in one package: moist salmon, savory mushrooms, bright lemon zest and capers, rich, flaky pastry. They're perfect for a dinner party, and what's brilliant is that you can prepare these the day before, keep them in the fridge, and bake them when your guests arrive. (You can easily scale this recipe up if you're having more guests.) I call for fairly small pieces of salmon because by the time you add the stuffing and pastry, each portion is ample. You need thick pieces of salmon, or they'll overcook. If you can only get the thinner tail end of the fillet, stack two pieces together to create a thick portion. If you use a food processor to chop the mushrooms, take care not to overdo it and turn them into porridge.

-------------------------- SERVES **4** --------------------------

1 Heat the oil over medium-high heat in a large skillet, add the shallots and a pinch of salt, and sauté until they're tender and fragrant, 2 to 3 minutes. Raise the heat to high, add the mushrooms, and season with salt and pepper. Cook, stirring frequently with a wooden spoon or other tool that scrapes the pan nicely, until the mushrooms have given off all their liquid, the liquid has cooked off, and the mushrooms are nicely browned, deeply flavored, and quite dry, 7 to 9 minutes.

2 Take the pan from the heat, let the mushrooms cool for a few minutes, then stir in the crème fraîche, lemon zest, dill, and capers. Taste and add salt and lots of pepper to taste—the stuffing should be highly seasoned. Chill in the fridge while you prepare the pastry and salmon.

3 On a lightly floured counter, roll out the pastry sheet to a 14-inch square. Cut the sheet into four 7-inch squares. Season the salmon generously on both sides with salt and pepper.

CONTINUED >>

4 Pile one quarter of the chilled mushroom stuffing on the center of one square of pastry. Set a piece of salmon on top of the stuffing. Moisten the edges of the pastry with a little water, then bring each corner to the center on top of the salmon, overlapping the edges a bit. Press firmly along the seams to make a tight, neat package; try to press out any bulkiness where the pastry overlaps. Repeat with the other ingredients.

5 Line a baking sheet with parchment paper or foil and arrange the salmon bundles on it, seam side down. Brush the tops with the egg wash and cut a couple of slits in the top of the pastry so steam can escape. Chill for at least one hour or up to 24 hours, loosely covered with plastic wrap.

6 Heat the oven to 425°F. Bake the chilled salmon bundles until the pastry is deep golden brown and lightly puffed and the salmon is cooked through (about 145°F on an instant-read thermometer), 23 to 28 minutes. Arrange each bundle on a dinner plate, whole or cut on an angle, with a pile of the greens next to it, if using. Drizzle the Lemon-Caper Beurre Blanc around the plate and serve immediately.

LEMON-CAPER BEURRE BLANC

¼ cup **fresh lemon juice**

1 tablespoon minced **shallot**

2 teaspoons finely grated **lemon zest**

½ cup (1 stick) very cold **unsalted butter**, cut into ½-inch chunks

1 tablespoon **capers**, drained and chopped

1 tablespoon chopped **fresh parsley**

Freshly ground **pepper**

Kosher salt

A Thermos is a great place to store a beurre blanc; it will stay warm and stable, so raid your kid's lunchbox!

MAKES ABOUT ½ CUP

1 Put the lemon juice and shallot in a small saucepan, bring to a simmer over medium-high heat, and cook until the liquid has reduced to about 2 tablespoons. Reduce the heat to low, add the lemon zest, and whisk in the butter chunks, one at a time. Keep the heat low so that the butter emulsifies into a creamy sauce rather than melts and becomes oily. Add the capers and parsley and season to taste with pepper and possibly salt, though the capers make the sauce quite salty. Keep warm.

GREEK-INSPIRED lamb, chard, and feta tourte

Full disclosure: This dish is not quick, but it is easy and so deliciously worth the time. And it's a meal-in-one—savory lamb, earthy greens, and tangy cheese all embraced by a double crust of flaky pastry; the only thing left to do is to pull the cork on a bottle of syrah. My tourte is a bit of a mixed metaphor, with its roots in English shepherd's pie, Greek moussaka, and, of course, French puff pastry, and it's all the more exciting for its many influences. If your store doesn't carry ground lamb, ask the butcher to grind some shoulder meat, which will have a higher fat content—and more flavor.

SERVES 6 TO 8

1 TO MAKE THE LAMB FILLING: Heat 2 tablespoons of the olive oil in a large skillet over medium heat. Add the lamb, breaking it up with a wooden spoon so there are no big chunks. Season generously with salt and pepper and cook until no longer pink, about 5 minutes. Scoop out the lamb and set aside. Pour off any grease.

2 Add the remaining 2 tablespoons oil, increase the heat to medium-high, add the onion, and cook, stirring, until very soft and fragrant but not browned, about 5 minutes. Add the garlic and cook for 30 seconds, then add the wine and boil until reduced to just a glaze, about 1 minute. Add the chicken broth, tomatoes and reserved juice, and rosemary sprig. Adjust the heat to a lively simmer and cook until it has a nice thick consistency, like marinara sauce, about 10 minutes.

CONTINUED >>

LAMB FILLING

¼ cup **olive oil**

1 pound **ground lamb**

Kosher salt

Freshly ground **pepper**

½ cup finely chopped **onion** (from ½ a medium onion)

2 tablespoons minced **garlic** (from about 4 medium cloves)

½ cup **dry white wine**

1 cup homemade or low-sodium **chicken broth**

One 14-ounce can **tomatoes**, drained (reserve ⅓ cup juices)

One 5-inch sprig **fresh rosemary** or 1 tablespoon dried

1 teaspoon **balsamic vinegar**

6 drops **hot sauce**, such as Tabasco, plus more to taste

¾ cup **fresh breadcrumbs**

⅓ cup freshly and finely grated **Parmesan cheese**

2 tablespoons chopped **oil-packed sun-dried tomatoes**

INGREDIENTS CONTINUED

3 Remove the sauce from the heat, and stir in the lamb, balsamic vinegar, hot sauce, breadcrumbs, Parmesan, and sun-dried tomatoes. Taste and adjust the seasoning with more salt, vinegar, or hot sauce. Refrigerate until chilled.

4 TO MAKE THE SWISS CHARD: Cut away the chard stems by folding the leaves in half lengthwise and slicing along the edge of the center rib and stem. Cut the stems across into ½-inch slices. Rinse well in a colander and pat dry. Stack a few leaves, roll into a loose cylinder, and cut across into ½-inch ribbons. Repeat with all the leaves. Rinse the leaves well in a colander and shake dry.

5 In a large skillet or Dutch oven, heat the olive oil over medium-high heat, add the stems, season lightly with salt, and sauté until they soften, 2 to 3 minutes. Add the leaves; if they won't all fit into the pan, just add a few handfuls, toss with tongs until wilted, then add the rest.

6 Cook the chard until tender, 7 to 10 minutes, then squeeze out the excess liquid by pressing the chard against the side of the pan and pouring off the juices.

7 Add the butter and toss to distribute it, then sprinkle the flour over the chard and toss to blend. Add the half-and-half and cook, stirring frequently, until the greens are coated by a nice creamy sauce, 2 to 3 minutes. Season with the ½ teaspoon salt, pepper, and a pinch of nutmeg. Taste and adjust the seasoning. Stir in the egg.

SWISS CHARD

1 pound **Swiss chard**, tough ends trimmed from stems

1 tablespoon **olive oil**

Kosher salt, plus ½ teaspoon

1 tablespoon **unsalted butter**

1 tablespoon **all-purpose flour**

½ cup **half-and-half**

¼ teaspoon freshly ground **pepper**

Freshly grated **nutmeg**

1 **large egg**, beaten well

2 sheets (about 9 ounces each) **frozen puff pastry**, thawed

1 cup crumbled **feta cheese** (about 4 ounces)

CONTINUED >>

You can make both the meat filling and the Swiss chard up to one day ahead, but don't add the egg to the chard until ready to assemble the pie. If your fillings are cold, increase the baking time by a few minutes to be sure everything is hot and the pastry is cooked. Reheat any leftovers on a baking sheet in a 375°F oven until the filling is hot, 10 to 15 minutes.

8 To assemble the pie, on a lightly floured counter, roll one sheet of pastry into a 12-inch square and transfer to a 9-inch pie pan. Trim the pastry to the edge of the rim of the pan.

9 Spread the cooled lamb filling evenly in the bottom, spread half the feta over the lamb, spread an even layer of the chard on the feta, and finish with the rest of the feta.

10 Roll the second sheet of pastry to a 10-inch square and cut a 10-inch round (using a plate or pot lid as a template). Lay the circle on top of the pie, pinch the edges to seal, and crimp to make a neat edge. Chill the pie for about 15 minutes.

11 Heat the oven to 400°F. Cut five small slits in a spoke pattern in the center of the pie to release steam. Bake in the hot oven until the pastry has puffed slightly and is nicely golden brown and the filling is hot, 30 to 40 minutes. Let the pie rest for 15 to 30 minutes before cutting and serving.

beef stroganoff in pastry cases
WITH SCALLION CREAM

Beef stroganoff is a 1960s classic that never really went out of style because everyone loves it. How could you not—beef tenderloin, sautéed mushrooms, and a tangy dose of sour cream? Yes, please. I'm serving it here in a puff-pastry case, rather than on a bed of noodles, because I love the texture contrast between suave stew and crunchy case. The stew is quite luxurious, so serve it with a simple vegetable, a few choice asparagus spears or some elegant green beans. I call for low-sodium beef broth, which isn't in every store. Don't substitute with regular, which will be too salty; instead, use low-sodium chicken broth. I cut the mushrooms in chunks and in slices because I want complexity in the texture (the slices get deeply browned while the chunks stay juicy and meaty), but if you're using already-sliced mushrooms, don't worry about this step.

------------- SERVES **6** -------------

1 TO MAKE THE SCALLION CREAM: Combine all the ingredients in a small bowl and let the flavors marry for at least a half hour, and up to 4 hours ahead.

2 TO MAKE THE STROGANOFF: Cut about half the mushrooms into ⅛-inch slices and the other half into quarters. Heat 1 tablespoon of the oil in a large (12-inch) skillet over medium-high heat. Add all the mushrooms, season lightly with salt and pepper, and cook, stirring frequently, until the mushrooms are lightly browned and most of the moisture has been cooked off, 7 to 9 minutes. Transfer to a bowl and set aside.

CONTINUED ▸▸

SCALLION CREAM

½ cup **sour cream**

2 teaspoons finely chopped **scallions**

1 teaspoon finely grated **lemon zest**

⅛ teaspoon **cayenne pepper**

¼ teaspoon **kosher salt**

STROGANOFF

12 ounces **cremini mushrooms,** wiped clean, ends trimmed

3 tablespoons **vegetable** or **olive oil**

Kosher salt

Freshly ground **pepper**

1 cup finely chopped **onion** (about 1 medium onion)

12 ounces **beef tenderloin,** cut into ⅛-by-1-inch slices

2 tablespoons **all-purpose flour**

2 tablespoons **tomato paste**

2½ cups low-sodium canned or homemade **beef broth** or **veal stock**

1 teaspoon **Dijon mustard**

------- INGREDIENTS CONTINUED -------

1 tablespoon **Worcestershire sauce**

½ teaspoon chopped **fresh thyme**

½ cup **sour cream** or **crème fraîche**

4 sheets (about 9 ounces each) **frozen puff pastry**, thawed

A few sliced **scallions**, for decoration

3 Return the pan to the heat. Add another tablespoon of oil and the onion. Reduce the heat to medium, season lightly with salt, and cook until soft, fragrant, and translucent but not browned, about 3 minutes. Transfer to the bowl with the mushrooms.

4 Toss the beef with the flour; season with salt and pepper. Add the remaining 1 tablespoon oil to the pan, place over medium-high heat, add the beef, and cook until lightly browned but still quite rare, about 1 minute. Transfer to the bowl with the mushrooms and onion.

5 Put the pan back on medium heat, add the tomato paste, and cook, scraping up all the browned bits in the pan (you're also "toasting" the tomato paste a bit for more flavor), about 1 minute. Add the broth, adjust the heat to a moderate boil, and cook until the broth has reduced to about 1½ cups. Whisk in the Dijon, Worcestershire, and thyme, then whisk in the sour cream. Turn down the heat to avoid a hard boil (which could cause the sour cream to curdle) and simmer a few minutes to let sauce thicken a bit. Taste and adjust with more salt, pepper, Worcestershire, or Dijon.

6 Return the mushrooms, onions, and beef to the sauce. Keep warm, but not over the heat (which could cause the sauce to separate).

7 Heat the oven to 400°F. Roll one sheet of pastry on a lightly floured counter to a 10-by-15-inch rectangle. Prick it all over with a fork at 1-inch intervals. Cut it into six 5-inch rounds and arrange these on a lightly moistened baking sheet. Take the next sheet of pastry and roll lightly to a 10-inch square; don't prick it. Cut out four more 5-inch rounds. Using a 4-inch cutter, stamp out the inside of each circle to create a ring. Repeat with the remaining two sheets, so you have a total of 6 solid rounds and 12 rings. Save the scraps for another use or discard.

8 Brush the edge of each round (which is your base) with water, then carefully lay a ring on top. Moisten the ring and top with a second one. With the back of a small knife, make vertical indentations all the way around the pastry at ½-inch intervals *(chiqueter)*, to help knit the two pieces of pastry together.

9 Bake until puffed and rich golden brown, about 15 minutes. Let cool on a rack. If the centers have puffed up a lot, tamp down with your fingers to create more space for the stroganoff.

10 When you're ready to serve, gently reheat the stroganoff and divide it among the cases. Top with a small dollop of the scallion cream and some sliced scallions and serve immediately.

------------   **DO AHEAD**   ------------

You can shape the pastry cases and freeze them up to a week ahead, and bake them up to four hours ahead. You can make the stroganoff up to a day ahead; gently reheat it in a skillet, adding some broth or water to thin a little if necessary.

desserts, cookies,
AND OTHER
sweet pastries

honey-ginger apple croustades
WITH CINNAMON-SUGAR WALNUTS

Croustade is just another way to say "rustic tart," but it sounds good, doesn't it? These individual croustades look so sweet on a dessert plate. And because they're rustic, there's no need to worry about shaping the pastry—just fold up a little border and you're done. I take these a step beyond a simple fruit tart by sprinkling them with crunchy glazed spiced walnuts, but they're perfectly lovely unadorned, too.

------------------ MAKES **6** 3½-INCH CROUSTADES ------------------

1 Heat 2 tablespoons of the butter in a large skillet over medium-high heat until sizzling, then add the apples and toss to coat. Sauté until a lot of the moisture has steamed off and the apples start to soften and brown, 8 to 10 minutes.

2 Add the honey, ginger, cinnamon, and salt and toss to blend. Taste and add more of any of these flavorings if you like. Set aside to cool.

3 On a lightly floured counter, roll the pastry into a 10-by-15-inch rectangle. Cut into six 5-by-5-inch squares, then trim off the corners of each square to make a rough round.

4 Heat the oven to 400°F.

5 Arrange the pastry rounds on a baking sheet and prick each one at ½-inch intervals. Portion the apple filling evenly among the pastry rounds, leaving about a ½-inch border of pastry. Wet the border with a little water and loosely pleat it to create an edge that embraces the apples; the pastry won't cover the center of the apple filling. Brush the edge with some of the melted butter.

CONTINUED >>

2 tablespoons **unsalted butter**, plus about 2 tablespoons melted for glazing

1¼ pounds **apples** (about 5 medium, I like Braeburns and Fujis), peeled, cored, and cut into ½-inch chunks to make about 5 cups

1 tablespoon **honey**

1 teaspoon finely grated **fresh ginger**

¼ teaspoon **ground cinnamon**

Pinch of **kosher salt**

1 sheet (about 9 ounces) **frozen puff pastry**, thawed

Cinnamon-Sugar Walnuts (recipe follows)

------------- DO AHEAD -------------

To make these ahead, fill and shape the croustades, freeze them unwrapped until firm, then wrap well in plastic and freeze until ready to bake. Bake directly from the freezer and add a few minutes to the cooking time.

6 Bake the croustades until the pastry is pale gold and set, about 18 minutes; brush a little more butter onto the pastry and continue baking until the pastry is puffed and a rich golden brown on the border and undersides (lift one to check), another 5 to 7 minutes.

7 Slide the croustades onto a cooling rack. Sprinkle each one with a heaping tablespoon of Cinnamon-Sugar Walnuts and let cool for at least 15 minutes or up to 1 hour before serving.

CINNAMON-SUGAR WALNUTS

½ cup **walnut halves**

2 tablespoons **granulated sugar**

Pinch of **kosher salt**

⅛ teaspoon **ground cinnamon**

These nuts are tasty for munching as well as for garnishing the croustades. Be careful when you're stirring because the sugar gets very hot.

-------------------- MAKES ABOUT **½** CUP --------------------

1 Line a plate with foil. Put the walnuts, sugar, and salt in a small skillet and heat over medium-high heat. Cook, stirring occasionally, until the sugar starts to melt but is not yet syrupy and the walnuts start to smell toasty. Don't let the sugar caramelize. Pour the nuts onto the plate, sprinkle with the cinnamon, and let cool completely.

2 Put the nuts in a heavy plastic bag and crush them with something heavy. You want small pieces with a little bit of powder. Taste and add more salt or cinnamon to taste.

peach and pecan tarts
WITH BROWN SUGAR TOPPING

I don't like adding extra steps to recipes, but I think taking the time to peel the peaches is a smart move: Dip the peaches in boiling water for 30 to 60 seconds, and then plunge them into ice water for 20 seconds—the skins will slide right off.

-------------------- MAKES **8** 4-INCH TARTS --------------------

1 TO MAKE THE PECAN CREAM: Process the pecans in a food processor until finely ground; don't go as far as making them a paste. Add the butter, powdered sugar, flour, salt, and vanilla and pulse to blend well. Add the 2 tablespoons egg and blend until creamy. Scrape into a bowl, cover, and chill until thickened and firm, at least half an hour.

2 Heat the oven to 425°F. Spray eight 10-ounce ovenproof custard cups (little Pyrex bowls, often sold in grocery stores) or ramekins with nonstick cooking spray or grease with oil or butter. You could also use a muffin tin, but the shape of your tarts will be taller and smaller.

3 In a medium bowl, toss the peaches, sugar, lemon zest, and salt together. Set aside. Roll one sheet of puff pastry into a 9-by-13½-inch rectangle and cut six 4½-inch squares. Roll the remaining partial sheet into a 9-by-4½-inch rectangle and cut in half to make two more squares.

4 Line each cup with a square of pastry with the corners pointing up and brush the pastry with melted butter. Drop a spoonful of pecan cream into the center of each pastry cup, dividing it evenly among the cups. Divide the peaches among the pastry cups and sprinkle with about a teaspoon of brown sugar. Bake until the pastry is browned, 20 to 23 minutes, then reduce the heat to 350°F, sprinkle with the chopped pecans, and continue baking until a knife tip inserted into the pecan cream comes out clean, 5 minutes. Serve warm.

PECAN CREAM -------------------------------------

⅓ cup (1½ ounces) **pecan pieces**

3 tablespoons **unsalted butter** at room temperature

⅓ cup **powdered sugar**

2 teaspoons **all-purpose flour**

⅛ teaspoon **kosher salt**

¼ teaspoon **vanilla**

2 tablespoons well-beaten **egg**

Nonstick cooking spray, oil, or **butter**

2 ripe **peaches** (about 1 pound), peeled and cut into ½-inch chunks

1 to 2 tablespoons **granulated sugar** (depending on sweetness of peaches)

1 teaspoon finely grated **lemon zest**

Pinch **kosher salt**

1⅓ sheets (about 12 ounces) **frozen puff pastry**, thawed

2 tablespoons **butter**, melted

3 tablespoons firmly packed **brown sugar**

3 tablespoons **chopped pecans**

101

apricot and gingersnap rustic tarts

I love these homey tarts, which are a cinch to make and can take advantage of any stone fruit, which are so wonderful for baking. Apricots, plums, and pluots are especially nice—their sweet but slightly astringent flavor mellows and deepens in the heat, and as the moisture cooks off, the texture gets slightly chewy. Take advantage of the palette of colors at the market and use a mix. I often see stone fruit paired with amaretti cookies, but they're not so easy to find, so I use good old Nabisco gingersnaps. Serve with ice cream.

------------------------- MAKES **6** 4-INCH TARTS -------------------------

1 Heat the oven to 425°F. In a medium bowl, toss the apricots with the sugar, flour, lemon zest, and salt. Set aside (don't do this more than 15 minutes ahead, or the apricots may give off a lot of juice).

2 On a lightly floured counter, roll the pastry into a 9-by-13½-inch rectangle and cut it into six 4½-inch squares. Arrange the pastry squares on a baking sheet. Brush each with melted butter. Sprinkle a pile of gingersnap crumbs in the center of each pastry square, leaving about a 1-inch border. Divide the apricots among the pastry squares, just piling them haphazardly in the center, no need to arrange.

3 Pull up all four corners of each square and pinch the points together in the center (they will come apart a bit as they bake). Bake until the pastry is puffed and brown and the edges of the apricots are slightly browned, about 15 minutes. Reduce the heat to 375°F and cook for another 5 to 6 minutes to ensure that the pastry is cooked through and the fruit is a little drier. Transfer to a cooling rack, dust with powdered sugar, if you like, and serve warm.

4 to 6 ripe **medium apricots** (about 12 ounces total), pitted and cut into ¼-inch wedges

1 to 2 tablespoons **granulated sugar** (depending on sweetness of apricots)

1 tablespoon **all-purpose flour**

1 teaspoon finely grated **lemon zest**

Pinch of **kosher salt**

1 sheet (about 9 ounces) **frozen puff pastry**, thawed

2 tablespoons **unsalted butter**, melted

6 **gingersnaps** (about 2 inches in diameter, I use Nabisco; about 1½ ounces), crushed into coarse crumbs

Powdered sugar, for dusting (optional)

103

plum tart WITH GINGER-ALMOND FRANGIPANE AND SUGAR-SPICE TOPPING

1½ sheets (about 13 ounces) **frozen puff pastry**, thawed

1 cup **Almond Frangipane** (recipe follows)

1 teaspoon grated **fresh ginger**

8 to 10 **Italian prune plums** (about 1½ pounds) or **other small plum**, pitted and quartered

1 tablespoon **granulated sugar**

1 tablespoon firmly packed **brown sugar**

1 teaspoon **ground ginger**

⅛ teaspoon **ground cardamom**

½ teaspoon freshly **ground nutmeg**

1 tablespoon **butter**, cut into small bits

This large rectangular tart looks so handsome, with its puffed borders and golden spiced-almond filling cradling rows of Italian plums with pale jade interiors and glossy indigo skins. The small Italian prune plum is ideal for this recipe because the slices are compact. Even when ripe, a prune plum won't get sloppy-juicy, which is a great trait for an eating plum but not a baking one. Feel free to use another variety, but choose ones that aren't super soft.

------------ MAKES **1** 9-BY-13-INCH TART TO SERVE **6** ------------

1 Heat oven to 425°F and line a baking sheet with parchment paper (in case the frangipane leaks a bit). On a lightly floured board, roll the whole sheet of puff pastry to a 9-by-13-inch rectangle and transfer to the baking sheet; this is the base of the tart. To create the rim of the tart, roll the remaining half-sheet into a 4½-by-13-inch rectangle. Using a straight edge and a pizza cutter or large chef's knife, cut the rectangle into 8 strips (4 strips that are 13 inches long and ½ inch wide and 4 strips that are 8 inches long and ½ inch wide; there will be a few scraps of dough left over).

2 Brush one long edge of the large pastry sheet with water and lay a 13-inch strip along the edge. Brush the strip with water and lay another 13-inch strip on top of the first. Repeat on the other long side. Brush one of the short sides with water and place one of the 8-inch strips along the edge, fitting the strip in between the edges of the two 13-inch strips. Brush the strip with water and lay another 8-inch strip on top of the first. Repeat on the other short side.

3 Stir together the frangipane and fresh ginger and spread the mixture inside the border of the pastry. Arrange the plums close together in 3 long rows, alternating the direction the plums face on each row.

4 Mix the granulated sugar, brown sugar, ground ginger, cardamom, and nutmeg together. Sprinkle the plums with the sugar and spice mixture and dot with the butter.

5 Bake until the pastry is puffed and brown, 17 to 20 minutes. Lower the heat to 350°F and continue baking until the tart is brown and a knife tip inserted into the frangipane comes out clean, 5 to 6 minutes more.

ALMOND FRANGIPANE

I love this filling for so many fruit tarts, especially peach, plum, apple, pear, and cherry. And a favorite of mine (but not everyone) is a tart shell filled with almond frangipane and prunes . . . soaked first in Armagnac, of course! Very French and very delicious. The frangipane will last in the freezer up to a month, so make a double batch and save half for later.

-------- MAKES **1** CUP --------

1 Process the almonds in a food processor until finely ground. Add the butter, powdered sugar, flour, salt, almond extract, and vanilla and pulse to blend well. Add the egg and blend until creamy. Scrape into a bowl, cover, and chill until thickened and firm, at least half an hour.

½ cup (2½ ounces) **slivered almonds**

4 tablespoons **unsalted butter**
    at room temperature

½ cup plus 2 tablespoons
    powdered sugar

1 tablespoon **all-purpose flour**

¼ teaspoon **kosher salt**

⅛ teaspoon **almond extract**

¼ teaspoon **vanilla**

1 **large egg**

------------ DO AHEAD ------------

You can make the Almond Frangipane up to two days ahead and refrigerate.

gingery peach berry galette

1 sheet (about 9 ounces) **frozen puff pastry**, thawed

1½ pounds **ripe peaches** or **nectarines** (about 3 large), pitted and cut into ½-inch wedges

1 cup **fresh** or **frozen berries**

1 tablespoon **granulated sugar**

2½ tablespoons **all-purpose flour**

1 teaspoon finely grated **fresh ginger**

1 tablespoon **unsalted butter**, cut into bits, plus 1 tablespoon melted

1 tablespoon **coarse sugar**, such as turbinado or Sugar in the Raw

Peaches are wonderful in this galette, especially rose-tinged white peaches, but with nectarines there is no need to peel the fruit. So see what's ripest and take your pick. You can omit the berries, but they're pretty and they accent the flavor and texture of the stone fruit. This galette shape is so easy and versatile that once you get the hang of it, you can play with all kinds of fruit—apple slices, pear chunks, raspberries, wedges of juicy plum. The small amount of flour will help thicken the juices released by the fruit and keep the galette from getting too soggy; adjust the amount of flour up or down depending on the juiciness of the fruit.

MAKES **1** 11-INCH GALETTE TO SERVE **6** TO **8**

1 Heat the oven to 400°F. On a lightly floured counter, roll the pastry into a 15-inch square and cut out a 15-inch round; it doesn't have to be perfect. Slide the round onto a baking sheet (it's fine if the edges hang over; you'll be folding them up).

2 In a medium bowl, toss the peaches and berries with the sugar, flour, and ginger, then pile the fruit onto the pastry round, leaving about a 2-inch border.

3 Fold the edges of the pastry over the fruit, pleating at even intervals as you go around. Distribute the butter bits over the fruit. Bake the galette until the crust is lightly golden brown and the fruit is beginning to bubble, about 20 minutes. Brush the crust with the melted butter, sprinkle with the coarse sugar, and continue baking until the pastry is a rich golden brown—including the underside of the galette—and the fruit is hot and bubbly, 15 to 25 minutes (depending on how juicy your fruit is). If the crust is browning too fast, turn the oven down to 350°F. Let cool for about 10 minutes before serving.

oregon berry tartlets

1 sheet (about 9 ounces) **frozen puff pastry**, thawed

½ cup **Almond Frangipane** (see page 105)

About 1½ cups **fresh** or **frozen raspberries, blackberries, marionberries,** or **blueberries**

Powdered sugar, for dusting

I've named these in honor of the crazy-good berry farming here in Oregon. From midsummer through early fall, we're surrounded by the fattest, brightest berries on earth, from blackberries on brambles in the park, to legions of marionberries at farmers' markets, to bushes laden with marble-size blueberries at the U-Picks on Sauvie Island. Wherever you get your berries (including the freezer case), taste before you bake. If they're tart, toss them in some sugar. The cups in my mini muffin pan have a 1-ounce capacity and a 2-inch top diameter. If yours are shallower and wider, you'll need to shorten your cooking time. Be sure to let them rest 20 minutes or so before serving; the flavors will be better balanced.

MAKES **18** TO **20** TARTLETS TO SERVE **6**

1 Heat the oven to 375°F. On a lightly floured counter, roll the pastry into a 14-inch square. Prick it all over with a fork at ½-inch intervals. With a 3½-inch round cookie cutter, cut out 16 rounds. Carefully lay the scraps on top of each other, reroll, and cut out as many more circles as you can; you should get another 2 to 4 rounds.

2 Tuck a pastry round into each cup of a mini muffin pan, pressing down firmly to secure it and pressing the pastry into the sides of the cup. It's fine to press together any folds in the dough. The pastry will come up a bit above the rim of the cups. Chill for about 10 minutes.

3 Fill each shell with about 1 teaspoon of the Almond Frangipane, then insert 2 to 4 berries, depending on their size. Bake until the pastry is rich golden brown and the frangipane looks puffed around the berries and no longer liquidy, about 20 minutes.

4 When cool enough to handle, but still quite warm, transfer the tartlets to a platter and dust with powdered sugar. Serve warm, not hot.

DO AHEAD

You can make the Almond Frangipane up to two days ahead and refrigerate, or you can assemble the tarts completely, freeze unbaked, and then bake directly from the freezer, increasing the cooking time a bit.

brown sugar and brandy pear turnovers

These old-fashioned pastries acquire just a hint of sophistication with the addition of dried cranberries and brandy (which you can leave out, if you like), so they can perform not only as an afternoon snack for children, but also as a dinner-party dessert if you team them with a scoop of vanilla gelato. Make a double batch and freeze half, unbaked and well wrapped, so you're ready for drop-in guests anytime.

-------------------- MAKES **4** TURNOVERS --------------------

1 Put the cranberries and brandy in a bowl and soak until slightly softened, about 1 hour. Melt the butter in a wide, heavy skillet over medium-high heat. Add the brown sugar and cook, stirring, until the mixture is bubbly, about 2 minutes. Add the pears and salt and cook until most of the pear juices have been cooked off, another 4 to 5 minutes. Add the cranberries and brandy and keep cooking and stirring until the pears are cloaked in a syrupy glaze, 3 minutes or so. Add the lemon juice and stir to blend. Put the filling in a shallow dish and let cool in the refrigerator.

2 Heat the oven to 400°F. On a lightly floured counter, roll the dough into a 12-inch square and cut it into four even squares. Put a quarter of the cooled filling into the center of a square, moisten the edges with water, and fold over to make a triangle, pressing out any air pockets. Seal the edges by pressing firmly with your fingers, then again with the tines of a fork to crimp. Repeat with the other squares.

3 Transfer the turnovers to a baking sheet. Cut two vents in the top of each turnover, then brush the top surface with the cream and sprinkle with the coarse sugar. Bake until the turnovers are puffed and deep golden brown all over (check the undersides, too), 18 to 22 minutes. Let cool for a few minutes, then serve warm.

2 tablespoons chopped **dried cranberries** or **cherries**

2 tablespoons **brandy** or **cognac**, optional

2 tablespoons **unsalted butter**

1 tablespoon packed **dark brown sugar**

1 pound **ripe pears**, cut into ½-inch chunks (no need to peel)

Pinch of **kosher salt**

2 teaspoons **fresh lemon juice**

1 sheet (about 9 ounces) **frozen puff pastry**, thawed

2 tablespoons **heavy cream**

1½ tablespoons **coarse sugar** or **crushed sugar cubes**

109

honey-spice walnut tart

4 tablespoons **unsalted butter,**
  slightly softened

⅓ cup **honey**

2 tablespoons **granulated sugar**

1½ teaspoons **ground cinnamon**

1 teaspoon **ground ginger**

¼ teaspoon **ground cardamom**

Pinch of **kosher salt**

1 **large egg**

1 cup roughly chopped **walnuts**

1 sheet (about 9 ounces) **frozen
  puff pastry,** thawed

I'm afraid this may be the ugly duckling of this dessert chapter: The tart is flat, the filling is brown, but boy, does it taste good. The ingredients call to mind the exotic flavors of baklava—sweet honey, bitter walnuts, cinnamon, and other spices—and it's super easy to make. A slice of this would be lovely with a compote of plums or cherries, or a scoop of coffee ice cream.

--------- MAKES **2** 5-BY-15-INCH TARTS TO SERVE **6** TO **8** ---------

1 Heat the oven to 400°F. Put the butter, honey, sugar, cinnamon, ginger, cardamom, and salt in a food processor and process until smooth. Add the egg and process until just blended. Add the walnuts all at once and process only until blended. The nuts should be chopped, but not so fine that the mixture becomes a paste.

2 Cut the pastry sheet in half to make two strips about 9 by 4½ inches. On a lightly floured counter, roll each strip to 15 by 6 inches. Prick one pastry all over with a fork at 1-inch intervals. Slide the strip onto a baking sheet, spread the center of the strip with half of the nut mixture to within a ½ inch of the long edges and all the way to the edge on the short ends. Fold the long edges over the nut mixture to create a border. Press lightly to stick. With the back of a table knife, make indentations into the long edges about ½ inch apart to crimp the border a bit and make it stick better. Repeat with the remaining pastry and filling.

3 Transfer the tarts to baking sheets. Bake until the filling looks slightly dry on top and the pastry is deep golden brown on the edges and underneath, 18 to 20 minutes. Slide the tarts onto a rack to cool. Cut into 3 to 4 pieces and serve just slightly warm. You can reheat these for a few minutes in a 375°F oven.

puffed doughnuts
AND DOUGHNUT HOLES

These aren't the kind of doughnuts to serve with your mug of morning coffee, but rather with a demitasse of *crema*-topped espresso for dessert. These doughnuts are more delicate than a true raised doughnut, and you don't have to fuss with yeast or rising times. I'm suggesting four different toppings, but feel free to invent your own. Be sure to have all your equipment and ingredients set up before you begin, because the frying goes fast and you need to pay attention. And please make sure your oil is very fresh and clean; don't use the stuff from last night's fish and chips.

MAKES ABOUT **15** DOUGHNUTS
AND **15** DOUGHNUT HOLES

1 On a lightly floured counter, roll out the pastry just enough to smooth it into a 10-inch square. With a 3-inch cookie cutter, stamp out 9 rounds, then with a 1-inch cookie cutter, stamp out the centers of the rounds. Gather the scraps and reroll; stamp out another 6 or so doughnuts and holes.

2 Lay several sheets of paper towels on a plate or tray; spread whatever topping ingredients you're using on another plate (for the powdered sugar and maple sugar versions, use a sieve to sprinkle the sugar over the doughnuts). Arrange these near your cooktop so you can move quickly from the hot oil to the paper towels to the topping.

3 Pour oil into a large, heavy-based saucepan to a depth of about 1½ inches and heat it to 400°F; use a deep-frying or candy thermometer to monitor the heat. Test the temperature with one of the doughnut holes: Gently drop it into the oil and fry, flipping constantly with tongs or

1 sheet (about 9 ounces) **frozen puff pastry**, thawed

1 to 2 quarts (depending on size of your pan) **canola, peanut, or other neutral oil** for frying

TOPPINGS

Your choice of:

1½ cups **powdered sugar**

1 cup **maple sugar**

1 cup **granulated sugar** mixed with 2 teaspoons **ground cinnamon** and a pinch of **kosher salt**

1 cup **granulated sugar** mixed with 1 teaspoon **ground cardamom**, 2 teaspoons **ground ginger**, and 1 tablespoon finely grated **lemon zest**

CONTINUED >>

111

a fork, until the pastry is very puffed and deep golden, about 2 minutes. With a spider or slotted spoon, transfer to the towels for a quick blot, then drop into the topping and roll around to coat, using a spoon to get the sugar everywhere, or sprinkling sugar all over with the sieve. (Be careful, the puff will be quite hot.) When it's cool enough to handle, taste it to be sure the inside is cooked enough—it should be moist but very airy and not doughy inside.

4 Continue with the rest of the doughnut holes, cooking about 5 at a time, then finish with the doughnut rings. Be sure to keep the oil temperature as even as possible. Move the pan off the heat if you need to cool it down a bit. Serve immediately, alone or with ice cream.

CHEATER'S *pains au chocolat*

Two 3- to 3½-ounce (85- to 100-gram) good-quality **semisweet chocolate bars**

1 sheet (about 9 ounces) **frozen puff pastry**, thawed

Pinch of **kosher** or **sea salt**

About 3 tablespoons **butter**, melted

A *pain au chocolat* is the highlight of any trip to my local pastry shop (if you get to Portland, Oregon, you must stop at Ken's Artisan Bakery). But as for making them myself at home? Forget it. Here, I cheat and use puff pastry. The result is different—not soft like a croissant, but still flaky and delicate. The pastry may unwrap a bit as it puffs, but that's just part of the drama. This treat is all about the chocolate, so use something good. Valrhona, one of my favorites, is widely available, as is Scharffen Berger.

MAKES **8** PASTRIES

1 Line a baking sheet with parchment paper or a baking mat (in case the chocolate oozes). Cut each chocolate bar into quarters to make a total of eight 1¾-by-3-inch pieces.

2 On a lightly floured counter, roll the pastry into a 10-by-15-inch rectangle and prick all over with a fork. Cut the rectangle in half lengthwise, to make two 5-by-15-inch strips and then cut each strip into quarters (to make a total of eight rectangles about 3¾ by 5 inches).

3 Position a pastry rectangle in front of you horizontally. Place a piece of chocolate in the center vertically, sprinkle on a little salt, and fold one side of the pastry to the center. Brush the fold with a little water, then fold the other side over and press along the center seam to seal, leaving the ends open. Arrange on the baking sheet and brush with butter. Repeat with the other rectangles. Freeze for about 15 minutes or refrigerate for about 30 minutes. While the pastries are chilling, heat the oven to 400°F.

4 Bake the pastries about 15 minutes, remove from the oven, and brush with more melted butter. Continue baking until the pastry is puffed and a rich golden brown, another 3 to 5 minutes. Transfer to a cooling rack and let cool for at least 10 minutes. Serve warm.

milk chocolate and hazelnut melts

So here's my homage to Nutella, the hazelnut-chocolate spread that lucky European kids get to eat the way we eat peanut butter. Good chocolate and real hazelnut butter take these melts (which are simplified *pains au chocolat*) beyond just being a snack for kids. My daughter, Charlotte, loves them, but so will anyone who has a soft spot for nuts and chocolate. Hazelnut butter is available in many grocery stores, often in the natural foods section. Serve these with a pot of French press coffee.

------------------------------ MAKES **8** MELTS ------------------------------

Two 3- to 3½-ounce (85- to 100-gram) good-quality **milk chocolate bars**

1 sheet (about 9 ounces) **frozen puff pastry**, thawed

3 tablespoons **hazelnut butter**

Pinch of **kosher or sea salt**

3 tablespoons **unsalted butter**, melted, plus more as needed

1 Line a baking sheet with parchment paper or a silicone baking mat (in case the chocolate oozes). Cut each chocolate bar into quarters to make a total of eight 1¾-by-3-inch pieces.

2 On a lightly floured counter, roll the pastry to a 10-by-15-inch rectangle and prick with a fork all over. Cut the rectangle in half lengthwise to make two 5-by-15-inch strips. Cut each strip into four rectangles measuring 3¾ by 5 inches.

3 Position a rectangle in front of you horizontally. Spread about a teaspoon of hazelnut butter vertically down the center and then place a piece of chocolate vertically in the center, sprinkle on a little salt, and fold one side of the pastry to the center. Brush the fold with a little water, then fold the other side over and press along the center seam to seal, leaving the ends open.

CONTINUED >>

4 Arrange on the baking sheet and brush the whole surface of each pastry with the melted butter. Repeat with the other rectangles. Freeze for about 15 minutes or refrigerate for about 30 minutes. While the pastries are chilling, heat the oven to 400°F.

5 Bake the pastries for about 15 minutes, remove from the oven, and brush with more melted butter. Continue baking until the pastry is puffed and a rich golden brown, another 3 to 5 minutes. Transfer to a cooling rack and let cool for at least 10 minutes. Serve warm.

bittersweet chocolate cannoli puffs
WITH DARK CHOCOLATE SAUCE

I've always loved the not-too-sweet ricotta filling of a good cannoli, which I've tried to recreate here. The flavors in this dessert lean toward Italy, but the pastry shell is pure French. It's fine to eat these puffs just as you would a filled cookie (meaning with your fingers), but I prefer to serve a pair of them on a plate, drizzled with the Dark Chocolate Sauce, and to eat them with a knife and fork, like a crisp eclair.

MAKES **16** PUFFS TO SERVE ABOUT **8**

1 In a medium bowl, stir the ricotta, 4 tablespoons of the powdered sugar, the rum, orange zest, vanilla, cinnamon, salt, and chocolate. Carefully fold in the whipped cream. Taste and add a touch more sugar, if you like, but the filling should be only lightly sweetened. Set aside.

2 Heat the oven to 400°F. On a lightly floured counter, roll the pastry into a 14-by-10-inch rectangle and prick all over with a fork. Cut the pastry in half lengthwise and then cut each strip crosswise into eight even strips.

3 Line a baking sheet with parchment paper or a silicone baking mat (for easier cleanup). Arrange the pastry strips on the sheet and bake until puffed and light golden, about 13 minutes.

4 Carefully take the sheet from the oven and sift the remaining 2 tablespoons powdered sugar over the pastries. Return to the oven and continue cooking until the pastry is nicely golden brown all over and the sugar has melted into a glaze, 5 to 8 minutes. Transfer the pastries to a cooling rack.

1 cup **whole-milk ricotta cheese**

6 tablespoons **powdered sugar,**
plus more to taste

1 teaspoon **dark rum** or **Grand Marnier**
(optional)

½ teaspoon finely grated **orange zest**

¼ teaspoon **pure vanilla extract**

¼ teaspoon **ground cinnamon**

Pinch of **kosher salt**

1 ounce (about ⅓ cup) finely chopped
bittersweet or **semisweet chocolate**

⅓ cup **heavy cream,**
whipped to stiff peaks

1 sheet (about 9 ounces) **frozen
puff pastry,** thawed

Dark Chocolate Sauce (recipe follows)

CONTINUED >>

DO AHEAD

You can make the pastries and filling up to one day ahead but store them separately—the filling in the fridge and the pastries in an airtight container. When ready to assemble, refresh the pastries for about 5 minutes in a 350°F oven and then cool before filling.

5 When the pastries have cooled, split each one horizontally with a serrated knife and spoon or pipe the ricotta filling onto the bottom piece. Replace the top. Arrange one or two on a plate and drizzle a ribbon of the Dark Chocolate Sauce around them. Serve within an hour.

DARK CHOCOLATE SAUCE

1 cup **heavy cream**

1 teaspoon **light corn syrup**

4 ounces chopped good-quality **dark chocolate**

2 tablespoons **unsalted butter**

Pinch of **kosher salt**

DO AHEAD

If you make the sauce ahead, you can very gently reheat it to loosen it, adding a few teaspoons of very hot water to thin if necessary. The sauce will keep in the refrigerator for up to two weeks and in the freezer for up to two months.

If you use one of the amazing dark chocolates available in stores now, this sauce is as good as dessert all on its own. The recipe doubles well and keeps well, so make a big batch to use for other desserts.

MAKES ABOUT **1** CUP

1 Bring the cream and corn syrup to a simmer in a small heavy-based saucepan over medium-low heat; do not boil. Whisk in the chocolate, a few pieces at a time, until well blended and smooth; this may take a few minutes. Remove the sauce from the heat and whisk in the butter and salt, whisking until the sauce is glossy.

"churros"

WITH CHILI-SPIKED MEXICAN CHOCOLATE SAUCE

I'll confess: I've never had a true Mexican *churro*, so these may be far from authentic, but they're delicious, and just the tiniest bit addictive. Fried puff pastry is incredibly light, unlike a lot of fried doughs, and dipping the sticks into the gently spiced chocolate sauce makes this tasty dessert playful, as well. Make sure you set up your work area as I recommend below, because the frying goes quickly and needs your full attention. You can make the Mexican Chocolate Sauce a few days in advance; just be sure it's fluid enough to dip the delicate churros into without breaking them.

-------------------- MAKES **20** FIVE-INCH CHURROS --------------------

1 sheet (about 9 ounces) **frozen puff pastry**, thawed

¾ cup **granulated sugar**

1½ teaspoons **ground cinnamon**

⅜ teaspoon freshly grated **nutmeg**

1 to 2 quarts (depending on the size of your pan) **canola, peanut, or other neutral oil** for frying

Mexican Chocolate Sauce (recipe follows)

1 On a lightly floured counter, roll the pastry lightly into a 10-inch square. Cut it in half lengthwise into two 5-inch bands, then cut each band across into 1-inch strips, to yield 20 pieces.

2 Lay several sheets of paper towel on a plate or tray. Combine the sugar, cinnamon, and nutmeg and spread on a plate. Arrange these near your cooktop so you can move quickly from the hot oil to the towels to the sugar.

3 Pour the oil into a large (at least 4 quarts), heavy-based saucepan to a depth of about 1½ inches and heat it to 400°F; use a deep-frying or candy thermometer to monitor the heat. Test the temperature with one piece of pastry: Gently drop it into the oil and fry, flipping constantly using tongs or a fork, until the pastry is very puffed and golden brown, about 2 minutes. With a spider or slotted spoon, transfer to the towels for a quick blot, then drop into the sugar mixture and roll around to

CONTINUED >>

coat. (Be careful, the churro will be quite hot.) When it's cool enough to handle, taste it to be sure the inside is cooked enough—it should be moist but very airy and not doughy inside.

4 Continue with the rest of the pastry, cooking about 5 at a time. Be sure to keep the oil temperature as even as possible. Move the pan off the heat if you need to cool it down a bit.

5 To serve the churros, stand them up in short glasses, pour the Mexican Chocolate Sauce into individual bowls for dipping, and serve immediately.

MEXICAN CHOCOLATE SAUCE

1 cup **heavy cream**

4 ounces good-quality **semisweet chocolate**, chopped

1 teaspoon **ground cinnamon**

1 teaspoon **pure vanilla extract**

¼ teaspoon **pure almond extract**

⅛ teaspoon **cayenne pepper**

------------- **DO AHEAD** -------------

You can store the sauce in the refrigerator up to two weeks or in the freezer for up to two months.

You might want to make a double batch of this sauce because there are so many delicious destinations for its deep chocolaty-ness with underlying notes of spice and nuts.

-------------------- MAKES ABOUT **1½** CUPS --------------------

1 Heat the cream in a small saucepan until it just begins to simmer. Remove it from the heat and add the chocolate, cinnamon, vanilla extract, almond extract, and cayenne and let sit undisturbed for about 2 minutes to allow the chocolate to melt. Whisk until everything is combined and the sauce is smooth. When you're ready to serve, if the sauce seems a little thick, whisk in a few spoonfuls of very hot water to loosen.

s'mores

Retro desserts are great for dinner parties simply because of the fun factor, but they're even nicer when you can upgrade them a bit from the childhood original. In this version, the warm and gooey filling is sandwiched between two flat, crisp wafers of puff pastry, which I sweeten with a dusting of cinnamon sugar. Kids might want a true graham cracker–size serving, but grownups will appreciate this smaller serving, perfect with a scoop of coffee gelato. I call for mini marshmallows, but large ones will work if you halve them so they're not too tall. Don't worry if your chocolate doesn't fit the wafer exactly—once it melts, you won't notice. Be sure to fix any weak spots in the seams of your pastry or you'll have trouble rolling out an even sheet (see **You Need to Know This!** page 7).

-------------- MAKES **12** 2¼-INCH SQUARE S'MORES --------------

1 Heat the oven to 400°F. On a lightly floured counter, roll the pastry into an 11-by-16-inch rectangle; don't worry if the edges are raggedy at this point, you'll trim them later. Moisten a baking sheet with a bit of water, and lay the pastry on top. Cover with either another baking sheet of the same size or an inverted heavy cooling rack that covers all of the pastry. Bake until the pastry is rich golden brown, 18 to 20 minutes. Remove the top sheet or rack, slide the pastry onto a cutting board and leave to cool, then carefully trim the edges so you have a 10-by-15-inch rectangle. Cut lengthwise into four 2½-inch panels, then cut each panel into 6 squares, to yield 24 squares.

2 In a small bowl, mix the sugar, cinnamon, and salt. Arrange 12 pastry squares on one baking sheet (these will be the bottoms).

1 sheet (about 9 ounces) **frozen puff pastry**, thawed

2 teaspoons **granulated sugar**

½ teaspoon **ground cinnamon**

Pinch of **kosher salt**

Two 3- to 3½-ounce (85- to 100-gram) good-quality **semisweet chocolate bars**

About 1½ cups **mini marshmallows**

1 tablespoon **unsalted butter**, melted

CONTINUED >>

3 If you've turned the oven off, reheat to 400°F. Break the chocolate into pieces and arrange on the squares (it's fine if there are some gaps), then arrange the marshmallows on the chocolate. Put the remaining 12 squares of pastry on another baking sheet. Brush these with the melted butter and sprinkle evenly with the cinnamon-sugar mixture. Bake the bottoms until the chocolate is starting to melt and the marsh-mallows have puffed and begun to brown, 4 to 6 minutes. After about 2 minutes, slide the pan with the sugared tops into the oven also and bake until the sugar starts to melt, 2 to 3 minutes.

4 Transfer a chocolate and marshmallow bottom to a plate and gently arrange a top to cover. Press just lightly to get the marshmallows to ooze a bit. Serve immediately, but be careful because the filling is hot.

DO AHEAD

You can bake the "graham crackers" up to one day ahead, as long as the weather's not too humid. Keep them in an airtight container. To make entertaining easier, you can assemble the s'mores, including the chocolate and marshmallows, on a baking sheet and then just bake until gooey at the last minute.

QUICK chocolate-raspberry napoleons

1 sheet (about 9 ounces) **frozen puff pastry**, thawed

½ cup **powdered sugar**, plus more for decoration

3½ ounces good-quality **semisweet or bittersweet chocolate**, chopped

2 cups **whipping cream**

1 teaspoon **pure vanilla extract**

⅛ teaspoon **kosher salt**

2 pints **fresh raspberries**

This stunning dessert is so easy to make, it's ridiculous. While a classic napoleon (also called a *mille-feuille*) has three pastry layers, this version has just two because I think it's so much easier to eat that way. The goal when baking the pastry is to brown it through without letting it actually puff. Kind of counterintuitive, I know, but the result is a wafer-thin pastry layer that's amazingly delicate and crunchy—a perfect partner for the billowy chocolate cream sandwiched between. Be sure to fix any weak spots in the seams of your pastry or you'll have trouble rolling out an even sheet (see **You Need to Know This!** page 7).

-------------------- MAKES **8** NAPOLEONS --------------------

1 Heat the oven to 425°F. On a lightly floured counter, roll the pastry into a 13-by-14-inch rectangle (don't worry if the edges aren't perfect—you'll trim this later). Prick it all over with a fork at ½-inch intervals. Slide the pastry onto a baking sheet (preferably with no edge), lay a sheet of parchment paper on top (if you have any) and then arrange another baking sheet that's big enough to cover the pastry on top (an inverted cooling rack will work, too) to prevent it from puffing. Make sure it's perfectly flat on the pastry and there are no gaps between the pastry and the sheet or rack. Bake until the pastry is very deep golden brown, 15 to 20 minutes. Take off the top sheet and the parchment, and using a sifter, sprinkle the ½ cup powdered sugar evenly over the surface. Bake for another 3 to 4 minutes until the pastry is nicely glazed. Carefully slide the pastry onto a rack to cool.

2 Meanwhile, combine the chocolate and ⅓ cup of the cream in a stainless-steel bowl set over a pan half-full of water. Bring the water to a bare simmer and heat until the chocolate melts. Whisk until smooth and glossy (it may look curdled at first), then whisk in the vanilla and salt. In a separate bowl, using an electric mixer, whip the rest of the cream until it forms soft peaks, and then whip in ½ cup of the chocolate sauce, a little at a time (you'll use the rest of the chocolate as a sauce). Don't over whip the cream or it will get lumpy.

3 With a large chef's knife or a pizza cutter, trim the pastry into 16 three-inch squares. Place one square, sugar side up, on a dessert plate. Dollop a generous ⅓ cup chocolate cream on top, nestle about a ½ cup berries into the cream, and top with another pastry square. Just before serving, sprinkle a little more powdered sugar onto the top pastry square, and drizzle the remaining chocolate over the tops (if the chocolate has thickened, thin it to pouring consistency by whisking in a few tablespoons of very hot water). Serve within 15 minutes.

lemon curd—blueberry napoleons

2 pints **fresh blueberries**

1 tablespoon **granulated sugar,**
plus more to taste

2 cups **whipping cream**

2 tablespoons **powdered sugar,**
plus more to taste

1 teaspoon **pure vanilla extract**

Pinch of **kosher salt**

1 cup **lemon curd,** such as Dickinson's

1 teaspoon finely grated **lemon zest**

1 to 2 tablespoons **fresh lemon juice,**
plus more to taste

1 sheet (about 9 ounces) **frozen
puff pastry,** thawed

Given how dressy and delicious this dessert is, it's amazing how quickly it comes together. I use lemon curd from a jar to keep things simple, but I freshen the flavor by adding fresh lemon juice and zest; use the best quality curd you can find, and of course, homemade lemon curd is always fine. You could play with other berries, especially blackberries, but be sure to taste the compote so you can add the right amount of sugar.

MAKES **6** NAPOLEONS

1 Set aside about 1½ cups blueberries and put the rest in a small saucepan, along with the 1 tablespoon sugar and a few drops of water. Simmer over medium heat until the berries release their juices and the juices thicken into a nice, thin compote or thick sauce, 7 to 10 minutes. Set aside to cool.

2 In a large bowl, whip the cream until it forms soft peaks. Add the sugar, vanilla, and salt and whip some more, until the cream holds firm peaks. You want a lot of body, but take care not to over whip, which would make the cream "curdy." In another small bowl, whisk the lemon curd with the lemon zest and 1 tablespoon of the lemon juice. Taste and add more juice if you like; the flavor should be fresh and tart. With a rubber spatula, fold about a quarter of the cream into the lemon curd and stir gently to blend, then pour the lemon mixture back into the cream and fold gently to blend. Chill for at least 30 minutes so the flavors blend and the cream thickens a bit.

CONTINUED >>

3 Heat the oven to 400°F. On a lightly floured counter, roll the pastry lightly just to smooth it into about a 9-inch square. Prick the dough all over at 1-inch intervals with a fork. Cut into three 3-inch strips, then cut each strip into 2 pieces to yield six 3-by-4½-inch rectangles. Arrange on a baking sheet and bake until puffed and a rich golden brown, about 20 minutes. Let cool and split in half horizontally.

4 To serve, put a dab of the lemon cream in the center of a dessert plate (to hold the pastry steady), then position one of the pastry bases on the cream, spoon a pillow of lemon cream (a generous ½ cup) on the pastry, pile about ¼ cup fresh blueberries on the cream, then cover with the pastry top. Spoon a ribbon of the blueberry compote around the plate. Repeat with the remaining ingredients and serve immediately.

------------- **DO AHEAD** -------------

You can make the lemon filling and the blueberry compote a day ahead. Give the filling a few gentle strokes with a whisk to combine any juices that may have separated.

roasted pineapple and ginger napoleons
WITH SALTED CARAMEL SAUCE

The classic French napoleon goes Hawaiian in this dessert, which teams juicy-sweet roasted pineapple with the seductive heat of ginger and the tang of crème fraîche. The roasted pineapple works as a quick dessert on its own, for nights when a full-on dessert is too much, and the Salted Caramel Sauce is worth having on hand for the occasional spoonful on its own, or any kind of dessert emergency.

MAKES **6** NAPOLEONS

1 TO ROAST THE PINEAPPLE: Heat the oven to 425°F. Line a baking sheet with parchment paper or a silicone baking mat (for easy cleanup). With a large knife, cut off the top and bottom of the pineapple and cut it lengthwise into quarters. Cut away the core and then cut each quarter lengthwise into quarters. Slice away the skin, lay the pineapple strips on the baking sheet, brush with the butter, and sprinkle with the brown sugar. Roast for about 10 minutes, then turn the strips and continue cooking until the juices are bubbling and the pineapple is golden brown, another 12 to 15 minutes. Let cool and then chop roughly; you should have about 3 cups.

2 TO MAKE THE GINGER CRÈME FRAÎCHE: Put the crème fraîche in a large, cold bowl and whisk or beat with an electric mixer until light and fluffy. The cream won't increase in volume as much as regular whipping cream would, but it should lighten up. With a rubber spatula, fold in the powdered sugar, candied ginger, and fresh ginger, and beat a few more strokes to blend. Chill at least 30 minutes for the flavors to blend and the cream to thicken a bit.

CONTINUED >>

ROASTED PINEAPPLE
1 very ripe **pineapple** (about 3 pounds)

2 tablespoons **unsalted butter**, melted

2 tablespoons firmly packed **brown sugar**

GINGER CRÈME FRAÎCHE
2 cups **crème fraîche** (or 1½ cups **sour cream** stirred with ½ cup **heavy cream**)

3 tablespoons **powdered sugar**, plus more to taste

½ cup finely chopped **candied ginger**

2 teaspoons very finely minced **fresh ginger**

1 sheet (about 9 ounces) **frozen puff pastry**, thawed

Salted Caramel Sauce (recipe follows)

3 Heat the oven to 400°F. On a lightly floured counter, roll the pastry lightly just to smooth into about a 9-inch square. Prick the dough all over at 1-inch intervals with a fork. Cut it into three 3-inch strips, then cut each strip into two pieces to yield six 3-by-4½-inch rectangles. Arrange on a baking sheet and bake in the hot oven until puffed and a rich golden brown, about 20 minutes. Let cool and split in half horizontally.

4 To serve, put a pastry base on a dessert plate, spread a thick layer of the ginger crème fraîche on the pastry, pile about a half cup roasted pine-apple on the cream, then cover with the pastry top. Spoon a thick ribbon of the Salted Caramel Sauce around the plate and serve immediately.

SALTED CARAMEL SAUCE

1 cup **sugar**

1 tablespoon **light corn syrup**

About 3 tablespoons **water**

¾ cup **heavy cream** or **crème fraîche**

1 tablespoon **unsalted butter**

¼ teaspoon **vanilla extract**

½ teaspoon **kosher salt**

What is it about the combination of salty and sweet that's so compelling? I can't get enough of it, especially when the sweet comes from a deep, just-on-the-edge-of-bitter caramel. This sauce makes more than you'll need for the napoleons (unless your guests are true caramel fiends), but it keeps well tightly covered in the fridge (up to two weeks, or up to two months in the freezer), so you'll surely find delicious uses for the leftovers.

-------------------- MAKES ABOUT **1½** CUPS --------------------

1 Put the sugar, corn syrup, and water in a medium, heavy-based saucepan over medium-high heat and bring to a boil, stirring just until the sugar is moistened and starting to dissolve. Let the mixture boil, without stirring but with an occasional swirl of the pan, until it is a deep amber, very fragrant with caramel, and you see just the tiniest wisps of smoke, 9 to 12 minutes. Be very careful because the caramel is extremely hot at this stage. Move the saucepan off the heat and pour in a small amount of the cream; it will bubble up furiously. Whisk in the remaining cream, a little at a time to avoid bubbling over, then whisk in the butter, vanilla, and salt until the sauce is very smooth. Leave to cool; it will thicken as it cools. Serve warm or at room temperature.

profiteroles WITH COFFEE CREAM, RICH CHOCOLATE-ESPRESSO SAUCE, AND TOASTED ALMONDS

Profiteroles are a classic French bistro dessert that elicits the same response from everyone: yum. Traditionally, they're made from small choux-pastry puffs filled with either pastry cream or ice cream, piled in a bowl, and drizzled with warm chocolate sauce. In this version, I use small puffs of deep-fried puff pastry, which has two advantages: it's quicker and simpler than preparing choux pastry, and the texture is crisp and ethereally light. I'm using a mocha-almond flavor theme here, but you could use plain whipped cream and chocolate sauce.

MAKES **36** PROFITEROLES TO SERVE **6** TO **12**

1 In a small bowl, stir the espresso powder with the hot water until dissolved. In a cold stainless-steel bowl, whip the cream until it holds soft peaks; sprinkle in the sugar, vanilla, salt, and espresso, and continue whipping until the cream holds firm peaks (be careful not to overwhip or it will look curdled). Using a rubber spatula, mix about a quarter of the whipped cream into the mascarpone, stirring until smooth. Fold the mascarpone into the remaining whipped cream until the mixture is smooth. Taste, and add a bit more sugar if you like. Transfer the cream into a gallon-sized plastic bag or a pastry bag fitted with a small plain tip. Keep cold.

2 On a lightly floured counter, roll the pastry lightly just to smooth it out to about a 9½-inch square. Cut it into 6 strips, then cut each strip into 6 pieces, to make 36 squares.

3 Lay several sheets of paper towel on a plate or tray. Pour oil into a large (at least 4-quart), heavy-based pan to a depth of about 1½ inches

2 tablespoons **espresso powder**

1 tablespoon very hot **water**

1 cup very cold **whipping cream**

3 tablespoons **powdered sugar,** plus more to taste

½ teaspoon **pure vanilla extract**

Pinch of **kosher salt**

½ cup **mascarpone,** stirred to loosen

1 sheet (about 9 ounces) **frozen puff pastry,** thawed

1 to 2 quarts (depending on the size of your pan) **canola, peanut, or other neutral oil** for frying

Rich Chocolate-Espresso Sauce (recipe follows)

½ cup **sliced almonds,** lightly toasted in a 350°F oven for about 8 minutes

CONTINUED >>

and heat to 400°F; use a deep-frying or candy thermometer to monitor the heat. Test the temperature with one piece of pastry: Gently drop it into the oil and fry, flipping constantly using tongs or a fork, until the pastry is very puffed and golden brown, about 2 minutes. With a spider or slotted spoon, transfer to the paper towels. When it's cool enough to handle, taste it to be sure the inside is cooked enough—it should be moist but very airy and not doughy inside.

4 Continue with the rest of the pastry, cooking about 5 at a time. Be sure to keep the oil temperature as even as possible. Move the pan off the heat if you need to cool it down a bit. Keep the cooked puffs in an airtight container until you're ready to fill, just before serving.

5 To assemble the profiteroles, snip about ½ inch from the corner of the plastic bag. With the tip of a small knife, poke a small hole in the side of each puff and pipe in about 1 to 2 teaspoons of cream. Pile the puffs into shallow bowls or onto dessert plates (3 to 6 per person, depending on your portion size), drizzle with Rich Chocolate Espresso Sauce, and sprinkle with the almonds. Serve immediately.

------------ **DO AHEAD** ------------

You can make the cream filling, sauce, and toasted almonds a day ahead.

RICH CHOCOLATE-ESPRESSO SAUCE

¾ cup **heavy cream** or **crème fraîche**

5 ounces good-quality **dark chocolate**, chopped

1½ teaspoons **espresso powder**

⅛ teaspoon **kosher salt**

------------ **DO AHEAD** ------------

You can refrigerate the sauce for up to two weeks or freeze it for up to two months.

This sauce is a natural for a scoop of coffee ice cream, so keep some extra in your freezer for quick desserts.

------------ MAKES ABOUT **1** CUP ------------

1 Heat the cream until it just begins to simmer. Remove it from the heat and add the chocolate, espresso powder, and salt, and let sit undisturbed for about 2 minutes to allow the chocolate to melt. Whisk until everything is combined and the sauce is smooth. When you're ready to serve, if the sauce seems a little thick, whisk in a few spoonfuls of very hot water to loosen.

sugar-crunch palmiers

⅔ cup **powdered sugar**

1 sheet (about 9 ounces) **frozen puff pastry**, thawed

3 tablespoons **unsalted butter**, melted, if using nonbutter pastry

2 tablespoons **granulated sugar**, plus about ½ cup for dredging

⅛ teaspoon **kosher salt**

These are standard fare in Parisian pastry shops, and they have a certain sophistication because they're so simple and elegant in form. They're also dead easy. You can bake a batch without thinking twice to serve with coffee after a dinner party or when a friend drops by. Some palmiers are, well, the size of your palm (though *palmier* actually refers to a palm leaf), but I've made these petite so you don't have to commit to eating a whole huge cookie, and yes, you may have more than one. Rolling the pastry in powdered sugar, rather than flour, is what gives these cookies their delicate crunch, but it can be a bit messy. Sugar is hygroscopic, meaning it attracts water wherever it can find it, so as you roll, the moisture from the pastry itself will come out. Just accept the fact that things will be sticky and keep dusting with more sugar and rolling. The results are worth it.

MAKES ABOUT **40** COOKIES

1 Dust your work surface with some of the powdered sugar, lay out the sheet of pastry, dust it with more powdered sugar, and roll, turning frequently and dusting with more sugar each time, until you have an 11-by-14-inch rectangle. (You may notice the dough getting sticky as the sugar pulls moisture from it; just add a little more sugar.)

2 Arrange the rectangle horizontally in front of you. If using nonbutter pastry, drizzle the pastry evenly with the butter. Mix the 2 tablespoons granulated sugar and salt together and distribute evenly over the whole surface of the pastry.

3 Fold both short sides so they meet in the center **Ⓐ**, then fold their edges again to meet in the center **Ⓑ**. Fold in half like a book, pressing gently with your palm to seal the two sides together **Ⓒ**. Wrap in plastic and chill for at least 20 minutes to firm up.

4 When ready to bake, heat the oven to 375°F and line two baking sheets with parchment paper or a silicone baking mat (the sugar gets sticky). Spread the remaining ½ cup granulated sugar on a plate. Cut the pastry into ¼-inch slices, dip both sides in the sugar, and arrange on the sheet about an inch apart. Bake until the sugar is lightly golden, about 10 minutes, then with a spatula (be careful, the sugar is very hot) flip each palmier and continue baking until deep golden brown and the pastry is no longer doughy in the center, 8 minutes. To be sure, break one open. Carefully slide the cookies onto a cooling rack and let cool completely. They'll get crisper as they cool.

DO AHEAD

You can wrap and freeze the pastry "log" for up to one month, allowing the pastry to thaw only slightly before slicing and baking. If the weather isn't too humid, you can store these in an airtight container for up to two days.

Ⓐ To make a palmier shape, start by folding the short edges so they meet in the middle.

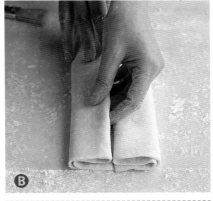

Ⓑ Next, fold the short edges to the middle again, keeping the edges lined up neatly.

Ⓒ Last, flop half the dough onto the other half. The sugar might get a little sticky, but that's okay.

sugar and spice spirals

3 tablespoons **granulated sugar**

2 teaspoons **ground cinnamon**

1 teaspoon **ground ginger**

¼ teaspoon **ground cloves**

¼ teaspoon **kosher salt**

½ cup **powdered sugar**

1 sheet (about 9 ounces) **frozen
   puff pastry**, thawed

3 tablespoons **unsalted butter**, melted

**These cookies are a homey version of a palmier, still light and crisp
but with an all-American spice mix of cinnamon, ginger, and cloves to
warm them up. See my cautions in Sugar-Crunch Palmiers (page 134)
about rolling the pastry in the powdered sugar so that you're prepared if
things start to get sticky.**

------------------- MAKES ABOUT **32** COOKIES -------------------

1 In a small bowl, mix the granulated sugar, cinnamon, ginger, cloves,
and salt. Set aside.

2 Dust the work surface with some of the powdered sugar, lay out
the sheet of pastry, dust it with more powdered sugar, and roll, turning
frequently and dusting with more sugar each time, until you have an
11-by-14-inch rectangle. (You may notice the dough getting sticky as
the sugar pulls moisture from it; just add a little more sugar.)

3 Brush the pastry with some of the melted butter, sprinkle with more
powdered sugar, and then sprinkle on about a tablespoon of the sugar
and spice mixture. Starting with a short end, roll the pastry into a loose
spiral, like a jellyroll. Slide the pastry into the fridge to firm up for about
30 minutes.

4 Mix the remaining powdered sugar, and sugar and spice mixture
together and spread out on a plate. Heat the oven to 375°F and line
two baking sheets with parchment paper.

5 Cut the pastry into thin even slices, between ¼ and ⅓ inch thick. Brush each side with a little more butter, then dredge thoroughly in the sugar mixture. Arrange on the baking sheets, allowing at least 2 inches between cookies. Bake until the spirals are puffed and the sugar is starting to caramelize, about 10 minutes. With a spatula, carefully flip each cookie and continue cooking until the pastry is completely cooked inside, 7 to 9 minutes. Let cool on a rack and serve immediately.

------------ **DO AHEAD** ------------

You can wrap and freeze the whole pastry spiral, then thaw slightly, cut, and bake. Or you can slice the spirals, lay them on a baking sheet, freeze until hard, and then pile the frozen slices into a freezer bag. To bake, dredge them in butter and sugar while still frozen and add a few minutes to the cooking time.

caramel-lacquered wafers

In French these are called *langues de boeuf*, meaning beef tongues, which is hardly an appealing way to describe these incredibly delicate, crunchy cookies. They start out like a classic palmier but then get rolled in more powdered sugar until they're as thin and soft as a piece of chamois. As they bake, the sugar melts into a shiny glaze and the layers of pastry don't puff, they just crisp. I love to eat them on their own, but they make a fun partner to a bowl of ice cream or any kind of mousse or pudding.

MAKES ABOUT **44** COOKIES

1 cup **powdered sugar,**
    plus more as needed

1 sheet (about 9 ounces) **frozen**
    puff pastry, thawed

1 tablespoon **butter,** melted,
    if using nonbutter pastry

2 tablespoons **granulated sugar**

⅛ teaspoon **kosher salt**

1 Dust the counter with powdered sugar, lay out the sheet of pastry, dust it with more powdered sugar, and roll, turning frequently and dusting with more sugar each time, until you have an 11-by-14-inch rectangle. (You may notice the dough getting sticky as the sugar pulls moisture from it; just add a little more sugar.)

2 Arrange the rectangle horizontally in front of you. If using nonbutter pastry, drizzle the pastry evenly with the melted butter. Mix the granulated sugar with the salt and distribute evenly over the whole surface of the pastry.

3 Fold both short sides so they meet in the center, then fold their edges again to meet in the center. Fold in half like a book, pressing gently to seal the two sides together. Wrap in plastic and chill for about 20 minutes to firm up.

4 When ready to bake, heat the oven to 400°F and line two baking sheets with parchment paper or a silicone baking mat. Dust the work

CONTINUED >>

surface with more powdered sugar. Cut the pastry into ¼-inch slices. With a rolling pin, roll each slice until it's a long oval, about ¹⁄₃₂ inch thick **A**. As you roll, turn frequently, dusting each side with powdered sugar, aiming to roll as much as possible into the pastry.

5 Transfer the ovals to the lined baking sheet and bake until the cookies are evenly glazed and deep amber, about 4 minutes. With a spatula (the sugar is very hot), transfer the cookies to a cooling rack. They'll crisp as they cool.

------------ **DO AHEAD** ------------

You can wrap and freeze the rolled "log" of pastry for up to one month, allowing the pastry to thaw only slightly before slicing and baking. If the weather isn't too humid, you can store these in an airtight container for up to one day.

These cookies are meant to be super thin, so roll the dough until it's really flat and floppy, rolling in as much sugar as you can so the wafers caramelize well.

index

acknowledgments

As anyone who's ever worked on a book knows, the author's name on the cover tells only part of the story. So many people contributed their talent and good humor to this project, and I'd like to share my warmest thanks with all of them, beginning with Amy Treadwell at Chronicle Books, who had the initial idea for this book. Huge thanks to my editor and friend Bill LeBlond, whose insight and encouragement got me started on this amazing journey. Also at Chronicle Books, thanks to Brooke Johnson, Jane Chinn, Peter Perez, and Amy Portello. I'm so honored and proud to be working with all of you.

Thanks to Ngoc Minh for the loveliest of photos; merci to Pouké and Christina for making my food look exquisite; and thanks to Alice Chau for the beautiful book design and cover.

On my team, a crunchy, crispy, buttery thanks to my brilliant and perceptive recipe testers, who never once complained about turning their ovens to 400 degrees on a hot August day: Sara Bir, Danielle Centoni, Kali Fieger, Nathan Hostler, and Woojay Poynter. I'm especially grateful to Ivy Manning for her help with development and to Shannon Wheeler, whose energy and sense of humor kept us going through some long days (the ice-cold rosé didn't hurt, either). Thanks to Li Agen for her laser-like yet elegant copyediting and to Kimberly Masibay for the beautiful buffing she provided, making me sound like me, only better.

table of equivalents

THE EXACT EQUIVALENTS IN THE FOLLOWING TABLES HAVE BEEN ROUNDED FOR CONVENIENCE.

LIQUID/DRY MEASUREMENTS

U.S.	Metric
¼ teaspoon	1.25 milliliters
½ teaspoon	2.5 milliliters
1 teaspoon	5 milliliters
1 tablespoon (3 teaspoons)	15 milliliters
1 fluid ounce (2 tablespoons)	30 milliliters
¼ cup	60 milliliters
⅓ cup	80 milliliters
½ cup	120 milliliters
1 cup	240 milliliters
1 pint (2 cups)	480 milliliters
1 quart (4 cups, 32 ounces)	960 milliliters
1 gallon (4 quarts)	3.84 liters
1 ounce (by weight)	28 grams
1 pound	448 grams
2.2 pounds	1 kilogram

LENGTHS

U.S.	Metric
⅛ inch	3 millimeters
¼ inch	6 millimeters
½ inch	12 millimeters
1 inch	2.5 centimeters

OVEN TEMPERATURES

Fahrenheit	Celsius	Gas
250°	120°	½
275°	140°	1
300°	150°	2
325°	160°	3
350°	180°	4
375°	190°	5
400°	200°	6
425°	220°	7
450°	230°	8
475°	240°	9
500°	260°	10